Motivating and Retaining Online Students

JOSSEY-BASS GUIDES
TO ONLINE TEACHING AND LEARNING

Motivating and Retaining Online Students

Research-Based Strategies That Work

Rosemary M. Lehman

Simone C. O. Conceição

JB JOSSEY-BASS™
A Wiley Brand

Cover design by Michael Cook
Cover image: © RomanOkopny
Copyright © 2014 by John Wiley & Sons, Inc. All rights reserved.

Published by Jossey-Bass
A Wiley Brand
One Montgomery Street, Suite 1200, San Francisco, CA 94104-4594—www.josseybass.com

Jossey-Bass books and products are available through most bookstores. To contact Jossey-Bass directly call our Customer Care Department within the U.S. at 800-956-7739, outside the U.S. at 317-572-3986, or fax 317-572-4002.

Wiley publishes in a variety of print and electronic formats and by print-on-demand. Some material included with standard print versions of this book may not be included in e-books or in print-on-demand. If this book refers to media such as a CD or DVD that is not included in the version you purchased, you may download this material at http://booksupport.wiley.com. For more information about Wiley products, visit www.wiley.com.

Library of Congress Cataloging-in-Publication Data

CIP data is available on file at the Library of Congress.
ISBN 978-1-118-53170-9 (pbk)

Printed in the United States of America
FIRST EDITION
PB Printing   10 9 8 7 6 5 4 3 2 1

Table of Contents

List of Tables, Exhibits, and Figure

TABLES

EXHIBITS

FIGURE

Preface

Participation in online education continues to grow in the United States (Allen & Seaman, 2010, 2011). However, concerns for online student retention and factors for student persistence must be taken into consideration. We know that among the reasons for student dropout are feelings of isolation, frustration, and disconnection; technology disruption; lack of contact with faculty; inadequate contact with students on the part of faculty; lack of student and technology support; lack of instructor participation during class discussion; lack of clarity in instructional direction or expectation; and lack of social interaction.

Based on the literature, we also know some factors that have a positive influence on retaining students and reducing dropout rates. Among these factors are previous experience in online courses, student preparation for online education, relevance of the course to students, learning community engagement, desire to complete a degree, and workplace support.

In preparation for writing this book we conducted a comprehensive literature review on student retention and persistence in online higher education. There was a dearth of information on strategies to retain and motivate students in online courses. To fill this gap in knowledge and expand on the existing literature, we conducted a study to investigate motivation and support strategies that could reduce online learner dropout in higher education (Conceição & Lehman, 2012, 2013).

THE FOCUS OF THIS BOOK

This book focuses on strategies instructors can use to retain online students in higher education. It offers design, student, and support strategies for instructors to motivate and support online students in institutions of higher education. This book is written for instructors from the point of view of both students and instructors. The main purpose of the book is to assist instructors when designing, teaching, and supporting the online experience of students.

WHO CAN BENEFIT FROM THIS BOOK

This book was written primarily for instructors to assist them in using effective strategies for online learning and teaching. By using these strategies instructors can better motivate and retain students in their online courses and successfully design and teach online courses. For new instructors, the book can serve as a practical guide for designing strategies to motivate and support students. Experienced instructors can use the student strategies in this book to guide students for more efficient and effective learning. Instructional designers and consultants, who work with programs and organizations, can also use this book as a guide when developing and administering online programs or assisting instructors when creating and delivering online courses.

OUR BELIEFS ABOUT LEARNING AND TEACHING

The strategies in this book emerged from an analysis of the student and instructor perspectives in our study, as well as our own experiences designing and teaching online for more than 10 years. Our thoughts about online learning and teaching are based on our core belief that education in general is developmental in nature. Students must be allowed to learn and grow at their own pace. Many of the courses we teach allow students to develop skills throughout the course period. Placing the student at the center of every task has been the hallmark of our teaching and writing. In the online environment, a learner-centered approach requires a sense of presence—in other words, a sense of the instructor's "being there" with online learners throughout the learning experience.

As educators we believe that we must take into account the unique nature of each student. Each individual is different in terms of past experiences, learning preferences, and interests. Therefore, we believe that instruction must be designed in ways that allow for individual differences. We always place ourselves in the role of a learner. Placing ourselves in this role helps us foster confidence, enthusiasm, and transparency in our teaching.

As our teaching experiences reach out to students globally, it is essential for us to teach using strategies that address different perspectives and provide options for the diverse learners. Having an open perspective about learning and teaching can help learners meet their own needs, think and reason more broadly, and select what is most relevant to them. We believe in intentional design, a method that involves purposeful actions and takes into consideration learner characteristics, the learning environment, and the teaching process. This book takes the view that intentional design is the foundation for developing courses that are successful at online student retention.

HOW THIS BOOK IS ORGANIZED

Chapter 1, "Concerns and Opportunities for Online Student Retention," addresses the challenges that higher education is undergoing related to online student retention. The chapter explains the causes for increased enrollment and the state of higher education and online learning. The chapter describes concerns for online student retention and opportunities for online education. The chapter also identifies new learner behaviors and skills needed to succeed in the 21st century. The chapter concludes with an explanation of the study we conducted to expand on existing literature, which served as the basis for our writing this book.

Chapter 2, "Design Strategies for Retaining Online Students," looks at intentional design for online courses, design elements and strategies to help students stay motivated online, and the impact of intentional design for online course success. The chapter concludes with design strategies for retaining online students.

Chapter 3, "Student Strategies for Staying Motivated Online," focuses on the strategies identified by the students for staying motivated in online courses and the pathway that emerged from our analysis of the study findings. The chapter also explains the study findings from a motivational perspective and concludes with a discussion of ways to incorporate student strategies into course design.

Chapter 4, "Support Strategies for Helping Online Students Persist," begins with students' perceptions about receiving support that emerged from our study and then suggests support strategies, with examples, to help online students persist with their courses and programs. Instructors can incorporate these support strategies when teaching an online course.

Chapter 5, "Pulling the Strategies Together," brings together the established findings and major contributions from our study related to online student retention. The chapter offers a model for instructors to help students persist in an online course and explains how to put the model into practice. The chapter discusses times of change for learning and instructors' skills for meeting students' 21st-century fluencies. The chapter ends with implications and conclusions for learning and teaching online.

ACKNOWLEDGMENTS

This is the third book in the *Jossey-Bass Guides to Online Teaching and Learning* series that we have co-authored. We continue to use the same enjoyable and rewarding process for writing our books. For this book, our writing process has become so natural that we often finish each other's sentences. This time, we met in person only twice, making use of mobile technology for communication, Google Drive for synchronous writing, and Dropbox for digital storage.

We are indebted to the students and instructors who participated in our survey and gave us insightful information based on their perceptions and experiences. Their insightful information will be a valuable resource for other students, instructors, instructional designers, practitioners, and administrators. We are also grateful to Tammie Rivera, who pulled together a literature review on student retention and persistence; the University of Wisconsin-Milwaukee Consulting Office for Research and Evaluation (CORE) for helping us with the quantitative data analysis of our findings, especially Professor Cindy Walker; our colleagues Johanna Dvorak and Chip Donahue for sharing their stories; and

Jennifer Freiheit, who reviewed the first draft of our manuscript. We are thankful to our editor, Alison Knowles, who provided us with support and trust as we worked through the book.

As always, our family members have provided us with patience, support, and the ability to distinguish between work and personal life as we wrote this book in our home offices. Most important, the accomplishment of this book has been the complementary nature of our expertise. We each bring unique knowledge, research, and practice in online education, educational technology, and instructional design. We truly enjoy working together and sharing our experiences with others. Our work continues through online conversations on our website, blog, Facebook, and Twitter. Look for us at http://www.einterface.me.

Rosemary M. Lehman
Madison, Wisconsin

Simone C. O. Conceição
Milwaukee, Wisconsin

About the Authors

Rosemary M. Lehman and **Simone C. O. Conceição** wrote *Creating a Sense of Presence in Online Teaching: How to "Be There" for Distance Learners* (2010) and *Managing Online Instructor Workload: Strategies for Finding Balance and Success* (2011). *Motivating and Retaining Online Students: Research-Based Strategies That Work* (2013) is the authors' third book in the Jossey-Bass Guides to Online Teaching and Learning series. The books focus on a learner-centered approach, provide instructors with sound strategies to teach efficiently and effectively online, and help instructors guide students to successfully complete their online courses.

Rosemary M. Lehman, Ph.D., is an author and consultant in the field of distance education and a partner in eInterface. She worked for 20 years for the University of Wisconsin-Extension, as Senior Outreach and Distance Education Specialist and Manager of the Instructional Communications Systems Learning Design and Outreach Team. In these positions, Rosemary taught online and supervised faculty, staff, government, and nonprofit personnel in selecting, designing for, and using distance education technologies effectively. She received her doctorate in Distance Education and Adult Learning, and her master's in Television and Media Critique, from the University of Wisconsin-Madison.

Dr. Lehman's research interests and areas of expertise include instructional design; synchronous and blended technologies; perception, emotion, and cognition at a distance; educational applications for media and technology; the development and integration of learning objects; and technology accessibility.

She has led numerous workshops on distance education, keynoted and presented at statewide, national, and international conferences, and was the recipient of the 2005 University of Wisconsin-Extension Award for Excellence in distance education and leadership.

Dr. Lehman authored *The Essential Videoconferencing Guide: 7 Keys to Success* (2001), edited *Using Distance Education Technology: Effective Practices* (2002), and co-authored *147 Practical Tips for Synchronous and Blended Technology Teaching and Learning* (2007).

Simone C. O. Conceição, Ph.D., is professor of Adult and Continuing Education at the University of Wisconsin-Milwaukee and teaches courses in the areas of distance education, use of technology with adult learners, instructional design, and principles and foundations of adult learning. She received her doctorate in Adult and Distance Education from the University of Wisconsin-Madison and her master's in Adult and Continuing Leadership Education from the University of Wisconsin-Milwaukee.

Dr. Conceição's research interests include adult learning, distance education, the impact of technology on teaching and learning, instructional design, and staff development and training. She was born in Brazil and has lived in the United States since 1989. Her diverse background brings an international perspective to the fields of education and training. She has researched and identified many aspects of good practice in online environments and is an expert in helping instructors and trainers understand Web-based technology tools, software, and design processes. She received the 2006 Early Career Award from the Commission of Professors of Adult Education from the American Association of Adult and Continuing Education.

She co-authored the book *147 Practical Tips for Teaching Online Groups: Essentials for Web-Based Education* (2000) and is the editor of *Teaching Strategies in the Online Environment* (2007).

Concerns and Opportunities for Online Student Retention

Higher education is undergoing major changes because of increased demands for flexible learning. To meet these demands, online education is developing as an essential mode of delivery and is transforming the educational landscape. This higher education transformation presents us with institutional and instructional challenges (Conceição & Lehman, 2011). These challenges bring into question the concepts of presence, communication, and interaction; redefine the characteristics of the higher education learner; and bring into play new ways of learning.

EVOLVING CONCEPTS OF PRESENCE, COMMUNICATION, AND INTERACTION

To help the reader become aware of the challenges and better understand the evolution of the higher education landscape due to technological advances, we suggest three institutional classifications that illustrate these changes: brick-and-mortar, brick-and-click, and click-link-and-connect. These institutional classifications explain the changing concepts of presence, communication, and interaction in higher education.

Brick-and-mortar is the traditional higher education environment, where learners live on campus and are present to others in a specific location; walk to classes; attend regular courses during normal working hours; participate in campus activities; and communicate, socialize, and interact with other students and instructors within the confines of the campus area (Conceição & Lehman, 2011).

Brick-and-click is the traditional higher education campus environment, where learners reside in campus housing or near campus, or commute with the advantages of the innovative use of technology (Carroll-Barefield, Smith, Prince, & Campbell, 2005). In this environment, learners communicate with others mostly via technology but also have the advantage of being able to interact with others face-to-face.

In this book, we are introducing the term *click-link-and-connect*, which describes a virtual campus environment composed solely of technology, where presence is elusive, communication is electronic, and interactions take place in cyberspace.

REDEFINING THE CHARACTERISTICS OF THE HIGHER EDUCATION LEARNER

Whereas the majority of *brick-and-mortar* students are traditional college-age students attending classes immediately after high school, some *brick-and-click* students may still live on or near campus or travel to campus but also take advantage of technology, giving them opportunities to better meet their learning and working needs. The *click-link-and-connect* students are those who do not live on campus but learn at a distance through a virtual campus. In this group, many of the students are nontraditional, older, place-bound, goal-oriented, and intrinsically motivated and have full-time jobs and family obligations (Dabbagh, 2007).

NEW WAYS OF LEARNING

Changes in the higher education environment and in learner characteristics call for new ways of learning. Modern technologies have provided the opportunity to learn anytime, anywhere, and at any pace, both informally and formally. Learning is no longer a part of a single formal setting—rather, it is everywhere.

Think of a mobile device that provides access to e-mail, the Internet, games, files, library resources, videos, music, blogs, social networking, and so on. Learning could take place through any of these applications in any location the user chooses. In this type of technology environment, the boundaries between informal and formal learning tend to blur, and students can lose focus.

Although it is more comfortable for students to interact in the informal environment, in the formal environment there is a need for purpose and guidance. With so many available applications, students can easily become distracted and overwhelmed and may lack motivation to accomplish course tasks. With proper direction on how to manage these ubiquitous technologies and focus on learning, students can be successful.

One of the major issues in online education has been students' lack of motivation to persist in their courses or programs. This chapter addresses this issue, as well as the causes for increased enrollment and the state of higher education and online learning. The chapter describes concerns related to online student dropout or retention and persistence in higher education and opportunities pertaining to these concerns. The chapter also identifies new learner behaviors and skills in the 21st century. The chapter concludes with an explanation of the study we conducted to fill the gap in knowledge about motivation and support strategies that could reduce online learner dropout in higher education. The study served as the basis for our writing this book.

CAUSES FOR INCREASED ENROLLMENT

According to Allen and Seaman (2010), institutions of higher education can have a positive influence on overall enrollments and on the increased need for online learning in the United States. At least three causes are generating increased enrollment in institutions of higher education: the economic downturn, market demands, and the exponential rate of emergence of new technologies.

In times of economic downturn, people tend to return to school. This tendency generates higher enrollments, with an impact on institutions' financial situations. Market demands can initiate competition, requiring institutions to reexamine their brick-and-mortar infrastructure and consider the brick-and-click option to increase enrollments and reach out to a wider population through online learning.

Another positive influence on overall enrollments is the rapidly changing development and use of technologies. The life of a technology today is very short and demands constant change and adaptation from users, who must learn new skills. Some advantages of emerging technologies in online education are the capability of creating presence, enhancing communication, and providing opportunities for interaction (Lehman & Conceição, 2010). People highly value these qualities in the face-to-face setting, and these concepts should be the basis for designing brick-and-click and click-link-and-connect environments. In these environments, higher education institutions are finding a new source of revenue without having to build additional physical facilities, recognizing increasing competition, and using emerging technologies to reach out to new audiences (Allen & Seaman, 2010; Maguire, 2005). One example related to this change is the advent of flexible degree programs that integrate MOOCs (Massive Open Online Courses) into their offerings (Ward, 2013).

THE STATE OF HIGHER EDUCATION AND ONLINE LEARNING

A 2009 report by Allen and Seaman (2010) shows that 66% of higher education institutions in the United States reported growing requests for new online courses and programs and 73% reported increasing demand for existing online courses and programs. This compares to 54% of growing requests for existing face-to-face courses and programs.

In an updated report, Allen and Seaman (2011) explain that in 2010 there were more than six million students (or 31% of students) in public, private, and for-profit institutions in the United States taking at least one online course. Participation in online courses has grown by 358% since 2003. Though the growth in online learning enrollments has been outstanding, there is still a misperception by academic leaders and faculty that learning outcomes for online education are inferior to those of face-to-face instruction. However, academic leaders at institutions with online offerings have a much more favorable opinion of the learning outcomes for online courses than do those at institutions with no online courses or programs (Allen & Seaman, 2011).

It is evident that online education still suffers from lack of knowledge of its potential by many leaders. In 2010, there was a small increase (2% over 2009) in the number of U.S. institutions of higher education reporting that online education is a critical part of their long-term strategy. In this instance, for-profit institutions are more likely to include online learning in their strategic plans (Allen & Seaman, 2011). Based on the 2011 report by Allen and Seaman, distance education continues to show growth. As a result, concerns and opportunities for online student retention must be considered.

CONCERNS FOR ONLINE STUDENT RETENTION

Online student retention has been a major topic of discussion in higher education for more than a decade. This discussion has focused on student dropout (or attrition) and persistence. Most articles have provided anecdotal information or individual studies carried out by universities (Angelino, Williams, & Natvig, 2007). In the past decade, there have been a few national reports on student enrollment, but none has focused specifically on dropout or persistence. What has been widely addressed in the literature is the comparison between the effectiveness of online learning and traditional learning.

Although studies support the effectiveness of learning online compared to learning in the traditional classroom (Hobbs, 2004; Tallent-Runnels et al., 2006), students often fail to complete online courses. In some studies, it is noted that as many as 50–70% drop out of their online courses or programs (Carr, 2000; Roblyer, 2006; Rovai & Wighting, 2005; Simpson, 2004). Among the reasons for student dropout are feelings of isolation, frustration, and disconnection; technology disruption; student failure to make contact with faculty; inadequate contact with students by faculty; lack of student and technology support; lack of instructor participation during class discussion; lack of clarity in instructional direction or expectation; and lack of social interaction. Another way to view the dropout problem is to look at the factors for student persistence in online education. These factors can help us determine what strategies are needed to retain students, reduce dropout rates, and help students persist in online courses or programs.

Reasons Online Students Drop Out

A review of the literature reveals many reasons for online student dropout. For example, Hara and Kling (2001) and Palloff and Pratt (1999, 2005) address the physical separation of individual students in online education as a reason for their feeling isolated and a major cause of student confusion and anxiety, leading to problems with course retention. The findings of Motteram and Forrester (2005) and Abel (2005) reveal that technology failure and lack of instructor feedback are also reasons for online student dropout. In the online environment, students tend to become frustrated when technology does not function well and lose confidence in their work when they do not receive instructor feedback. For these reasons, technology and student support are essential.

One way for providing support for students is through contact. Motteram and Forrester (2005) say that students rate contact with faculty as more important than contact with other students. Contact can be either proactive or reactive (Simpson, 2004). While proactive contact or intervention means "taking the initiative to contact students either in a teaching or an advisory environment" (p. 80), reactive contact involves responding to student-initiated communication. Proactive contact with a student or interventions from the institution can have an impact on the retention of online learners. Although both proactive contact and reactive contact are important, proactive contact is gaining more attention because students who do not make contact with available systems may be more likely to drop out (Simpson, 2004).

Another way to support students is related to instructor assistance. Chyung and Vachon (2005) found that lack of instructor participation during class discussion and lack of clarity in instructional direction or expectations can cause confusion and frustration and are reasons that students drop out. Inadequate assistance from instructors can also create student dissatisfaction in the online environment and has implications for student retention.

Other reasons that online students drop out were described by Muilenburg and Berge (2005), who identified eight barriers to online learning. We grouped the eight barriers into three categories: skill level, motivation, and support. In Muilenburg and Berge's study, students identified the barriers to their skill level as academic and technical. In the academic area they lacked skills in reading, writing, or communication. In the area of technical skills they feared the use of new tools and software and their unfamiliarity with technical tools for online learning.

Motivation barriers were intrinsic and extrinsic. Intrinsic motivation barriers included the characteristics of procrastination, selecting easier aspects of an assignment to complete, or the feeling that the online learning environment was not innately motivating. Extrinsic motivation barriers involved social interaction in which the students felt a lack of peer collaboration online, absence of social cues, or fear of isolation in online courses (Muilenburg & Berge, 2005).

In the area of support, administrative, financial, and technical issues were considered barriers (Muilenburg & Berge, 2005). Administrative issues emerged when administration had control over course materials and the materials were not delivered on time, when academic advisors were not adequately available online, and when there was a lack of timely instructor feedback. Financial barriers occurred when access to the Internet was too expensive. Technical issues arose when there was a lack of consistent platforms, browsers, and software; in addition, a lack of technical assistance caused obstacles to learning.

The barriers cited in Muilenburg and Berge's (2005) study are basic reasons for online student dropout. These reasons can create student frustration, dissatisfaction, lack of confidence, loss of focus, and lack of motivation and have implications for the ability of students to persist in online courses and program. Table 1.1 summarizes the common reasons for online student dropout and how they affect students.

Factors for Student Persistence in Online Education

Persistence means continuing decisively on a course of action in spite of difficulty or opposition. Findings from several studies of student persistence in online higher education have helped us look at the factors involved in retaining students and reducing dropout rates. One model that struck us in looking at persistence in the online environment was Rovai's (2003) composite persistence model, a combination of other models related to persistence.

In his model, Rovai (2003) includes the following elements: student characteristics and student skills (prior to admission) and external and internal factors (after admission). Using this model, institutions can detect students who are at risk to become dropouts and determine intervention methods. For example, if an institution knows the deficiencies in an online student's academic preparation and skills prior to admitting the student, the institution can rectify these deficiencies with early intervention.

Table 1.1. Common Reasons for Online Student Dropout

Common Reasons for Online Student Dropout	How Reasons Affect Students
Physical separation	Feeling of isolation and disconnection
Low academic skill level	Leading to remediation in reading, writing, or communication
Low technical skill level	Fearing technology and new software
Lack of intrinsic motivation	Leading to procrastination
Lack of extrinsic motivation	Feeling of isolation
Lack of faculty contact with student	Leading to dissatisfaction
Lack of clarity in direction	Leading to loss of focus
Lack of expectation	Feeling of confusion
Technology failure	Feeling of frustration and loss of confidence
Lack of administrative, financial, and technical support	Causing obstacles to learning
Lack of instructor feedback	Feeling of frustration and loss of confidence

Once a student is enrolled in an online program, the model can be used to recognize external factors to help with student persistence. External factors include nonschool issues that conflict with academic life, such as financial need or child care arrangements. Internal factors are affected by the student's needs and include consistency and clarity of online programs, policies, and procedures; self-esteem; feeling of identity with the school; social integration; and ready access to support services.

One study that addresses persistence from the student's perspective on online participation is Tello's (2007). His study found that student perceptions about their contributions in asynchronous discussion forums and students' frequent use of the forums accounted for 26% of the variance in course persistence rates. This finding shows that the interactive strategies used in the course affected student attitudes and helps explain why students persist or withdraw from online courses.

Another study that caught our attention was Müller's (2008) investigation of undergraduate and graduate women learners' persistence in online degree-completion programs. Her findings suggest that multiple responsibilities and insufficient interaction with faculty, technology, and coursework are the major factors for women's lack of persistence. However, motivation to complete degrees, engagement with the learning community, and gratitude for the convenience of completing a degree online supported persistence. It appears that a learning community approach in an online course or program can be a strategy for retaining students (Brown, 2001).

Park and Choi's (2009) study on factors influencing adult learners' decision to drop out or persist in online learning revealed that persistent learners and dropouts differ in their individual characteristics, course design factors, and workplace support factors. In their study, females accounted for 74.5% of persistent learners and 65.3% of dropouts. Learners in both groups ranged in age from 20 to 39 years old. In the dropout group, age ranged between 20 and 29 years old, the equivalent of 26.5%. Their findings showed that by addressing course design, such as enhancing the relevance of the course, institutions could have lower dropout rates. The results also indicated that adult learners need support from their workplace to persist in and complete their online courses.

Another study that addressed factors in online student persistence was McGivney's (2009) investigation of the persistence of online adult students in two community colleges. This study showed that the strongest predictors of course completion were the desire to complete a degree, previous experience in online courses, and assignment completion. These findings give us clues about how important it is to understand learners' characteristics and how prepared students are for the online environment to help them persist in their online courses and programs.

Rovai's (2003) composite model provides us with a framework to create an environment conducive to a successful online learning experience. It is critical for institutions to recognize student characteristics and skills prior to admitting a student to an online program. As McGivney's (2009) findings indicate, previous experience in online courses is a predictor of persistence. It is also essential for institutions to be aware of factors that influence student academic life. Müller's (2008) findings cite students' multiple responsibilities, and Park and Choi's (2009) findings address the importance of workplace support. These factors influence how well a student can do after admission to an online program.

The internal factors in Rovai's (2003) composite model encompass institutional interventions and are the ones over which institutions have the most control. Institutional interventions are based on student needs, pedagogy, and institutional support, which can be translated into design, instructional, and support strategies in the classroom. Based on the persistence literature, there is no simple formula to guarantee student success in online learning, because success involves a variety of factors. Institutions control the services they provide, but not external factors. When factors external to the institution come into play with factors internal to the institution, however, the institution needs to understand its learners, use appropriate strategies, and provide effective support in order to retain students and avoid dropout.

OPPORTUNITIES FOR ONLINE EDUCATION

Online learning in higher education presents concerns, but also opportunities. These opportunities can be turned into benefits for students who take advantage of them. Some of the benefits that online education provides are better access, convenience, flexibility, efficiency, creative risk, community building, connection with others without boundaries, and a green environment (Conceição & Lehman, 2011). Students who would otherwise be unable to further their education can have better access through online learning. Online learning is convenient for those who work full time and have families, because students do not need to travel to a physical institution and can work their courses around their own schedules.

Online learning has been called "anytime, anywhere, any pace education," a description that highlights the flexibility online learning provides to learners. With the advance of technology, we suggest an additional term: "any way education." Because of the proliferation of innovative technologies available today, students can learn any way they want. For example, students can take an online course that may include using a smartphone, a tablet, a computer, a personal digital assistant (PDA), a global positioning system (GPS), a smart TV, and so on. This versatility provides multiple opportunities for students to learn.

Technology can provide the opportunity to expand knowledge and extend the reach to people and places never considered before. Technology can make it possible to save time, travel, and cost. Technology can help avoid the necessity to take chances by traveling to other locations. Taking creative risks can provide opportunities for students to learn in new ways. Participating in virtual communities, social networking, and 3D environments allows for thinking, feeling, and acting as though students were face-to-face. These online environments connect students to diverse people globally and bring them closer together in communities that are no longer limited to physical places. Students can become psychologically and mentally present with one another without boundaries (Lehman & Conceição, 2010).

Finally, online education can be a benefit for a green environment because it allows students to store information and knowledge in digital devices and carry them and other "green" technologies anywhere. These benefits are not all-inclusive, but they provide a starting point for why online education can be valuable in the 21st century.

In this book, we suggest three institutional classifications based on changes that have transformed the higher education landscape: brick-and-mortar, brick-and-click, and click-link-and-connect. The changes are caused by the economic downturn, market demands, and the exponential emergence of technologies. These causes have impacted the state of higher education and online learning, bringing concerns and opportunities. The concerns can help us see the potential impact of online learning and the possible opportunities for online education. As online courses continue to grow in number, it is essential to provide quality course design, exemplary instructional strategies, and strong support to increase online student retention. It is also important to understand students' characteristics and the new learner behaviors and skills needed to survive in the 21st century.

NEW LEARNER BEHAVIORS AND SKILLS IN THE 21ST CENTURY

The ECAR National Study of Undergraduate Students and Information Technology (EDUCAUSE, 2011) provides significant data related to student technology ownership, use, and value in the United States. Today, 9 in 10 students own laptops, more than half have smartphones, and 1 in 10 possesses a tablet. When it comes to technology use and value, students state that technology provides them with easy access to resources and assists them with their administrative tasks and with tracking their academic progress. The results are a more productive academic life and an increased feeling of being connected and engaged in an immersive, relevant experience. Data confirm that student behaviors have changed due to technology usage.

More than a decade ago studies showed that typical online learners were between the ages of 22 and 50 years old, nontraditional, and enrolled in online programs because of work and family responsibilities (Dutton, Dutton, & Perry, 2002). These learners were self-motivated and preferred independent learning (Diaz & Bontenbal, 2001).

A more recent report by Aslanian and Clinefelter (2012) concerning 1,500 prospective and current online students in the United States shows a different online learner profile. Key findings in this report suggest that now individuals from a variety of age groups are taking online courses (40% are younger than 30 years old; 1 in 5 is younger than 25 years old). As high school students and traditional-age college students become more experienced with online education, the percentage of students 30 years and younger will increase.

Although students are interested in online degree programs, certificates will be the most attractive and their popularity is likely to grow. Students enrolled in online programs prefer a nearby campus or service center (within 100 miles) for their online studies. Transfer credits are common to most undergraduate online students prior to entering the intended institution (Aslanian & Clinefelter, 2012).

The changes in student characteristics and behavior go along with the interest in a compressed or flex-degree program of study for a reasonable cost at a reputable institution. For example, in the state of Wisconsin, the University of Wisconsin Flexible Option offers an accessible and inexpensive alternative for earning a degree. This option provides a portfolio of degrees, certificates, and courses, primarily from existing programs, offered through self-paced and competency-based formats (Ward, 2013).

Another online learning option that is being explored by higher education is the emergence of MOOCs (Massive Open Online Courses). The goal of

MOOCs is to reach out to a large number of participants through open Web access. Initially, MOOCs were offered free of charge; students took MOOCs to learn something new for the sake of learning or to prepare for a competency test. Today, in addition to taking some MOOCs without charge, participants may pay a fee for courses that lead to a certificate or degree (Waldrop, 2013).

Changes in student behavior due to technology usage also bring new demands for learning and teaching and new skills to function successfully in the culture of the 21st century. According to Carr (2011), "technology isn't the problem anymore, but what to do with it" (p. 68). Jukes, McCain, and Crockett (2010) suggest five student fluencies (or skills) needed to succeed in the new learning environment: solution, information, collaboration, creativity, and media. Solution skills consist of creativity and problem-solving skills applied in real life. Information skills give one the ability to access raw data using textbooks, cell phones, wikis, social networks, and other digital and nontraditional sources, images, sound, and video, as well as the ability to gather information and critically evaluate the data found.

Collaboration fluency comprises the ability to work online with virtual and real partners to produce original artifacts. Creativity is the process of being innovative through design, art, and storytelling. Media fluency involves two elements: (1) the ability to analyze and interpret the message of communication media, determine how to select media, and evaluate the usefulness of the message, and (2) the ability to develop and publish original digital artifacts, determining the most appropriate medium for a message (Jukes, McCain, & Crockett, 2010).

With changes in student population behaviors and increased demands for online learning in higher education, there is a need to explore ways to retain students and help them persist in the online classroom. Based on our own experience in administering programs and teaching online, we were concerned about student retention. Our first step was to conduct an extensive library, database, and Web search for empirical studies on online student retention in higher education. In our literature review, we conducted a search by using the terms "student retention, persistence, and motivation"; "online learning and teaching"; "online education"; and "online course design strategies and support," along with a few variations. We focused our search primarily on studies and reports ranging from 2002 to 2012. We found 41 empirical studies and four study reports.

We also found a few books related to retention in higher education, but no books related to retention in the online environment. We found a number of research-based manuscripts pertinent to student retention and persistence in online education, published between 1999 and 2001. We found no practical books detailing specific strategies to overcome the barriers influencing student retention and dropout in the online environment. At the time of our writing this book, the few books and manuscripts we found provided surface information and did not address the topic in depth.

FILLING THE GAP: STRATEGIES FOR ONLINE PERSISTENCE

To fill the gap in knowledge related to online student motivation and retention strategies, we decided to expand on the existing literature by conducting a study (Conceição & Lehman, 2012; 2013). Our study investigated students' strategies for staying motivated online and instructors' strategies for supporting students and helping them persist in their online courses. Data were collected by surveying higher education students (n = 439) and instructors (n = 60). Students completed a survey (see Appendix 1) addressing strategies that motivated and supported their online learning. Instructors completed a survey (see Appendix 2) addressing strategies they used to motivate and support their online students. Using purposeful sampling nationwide, we recruited students in higher education who had taken at least one online course and instructors who had taught at least two online courses.

Participants in the study included students and instructors from 10 disciplines: art, library and information studies, social work/criminal justice, engineering, business, architecture, nursing, health sciences, humanities, and education. Survey results provided descriptive statistics and qualitative comments. We used the constant comparative analysis method to compare incidents to other incidents, incidents to categories, and categories to other categories (Creswell, 1998). Coding of data involved looking for themes and patterns. The two different sets of participant surveys were used to triangulate data, allowing us to cross-examine the data from different perspectives.

The demographic information showed that of the student respondents, 62% were undergraduates and 38% graduate students. Of the instructor respondents, 27% taught undergraduate courses, 33% graduate courses, and 40% taught both. Course duration showed that 85% of the students attended 15–16 week courses, 21% attended 8-week courses, 15% attended 6-week courses, 15% attended 4-week courses, and 7% responded "other." Course duration for instructors indicated that 94% taught 15–16 week courses, 15% taught 8-week courses, 18% taught 6-week courses, 9% taught 4-week courses, and 7% responded "other." Among the student respondents, 50% had previously taken four or more courses. Among the instructor respondents, 67% had previously taught four or more courses. Table 1.2 provides a summary of participants' demographics.

Table 1.2. Study Participants' Demographics

Students (n = 439)	Instructors (n = 60)
Course level	**Course level**
62% undergraduate	27% taught undergraduate courses
38% graduate	33% taught graduate courses
	40% taught undergrad and grad courses
Course duration	**Course duration**
85% 15–16 weeks	94% 15–16 weeks
21% 8 weeks	15% 8 weeks
15% 6 weeks	18% 6 weeks
15% 4 weeks	9% 4 weeks
7% other	7% other
Number of courses taken	**Number of courses taught**
16% 1	6% 1
18% 2	22% 2
16% 3	4% 3
50% 4 or more	67% 4 or more

Based on the analysis of the survey responses and our own experiences, the next three chapters are organized into types of strategies used by students and instructors. Chapter 2 focuses on design strategies for retaining online students, Chapter 3 addresses student strategies for staying motivated online, and Chapter 4 identifies support strategies for helping online students persist. The last chapter in this book brings all these strategies together and offers our Persistence Model for Online Student Retention.

Design Strategies for Retaining Online Students

Designing for online instruction is different from designing for face-to-face teaching. The differences involve space, time, boundaries, use of the senses, level of interaction, level of planning, teaching effort, and so on. When we teach in a face-to-face classroom, we are in the same space with our students. In the online environment, we are not; the online learning space is elusive and requires psychological, cognitive, and emotional connection to feel, think, and behave in a way that is appropriate for the online environment (Lehman & Conceição, 2010).

In the face-to-face classroom, we have a clear sense of time; in the online classroom, time is a flexible concept. When we teach in a face-to-face environment, we have our learners with us in the same location, whereas in the virtual environment we are present with each other without geographical boundaries. When it comes to our senses, in the face-to-face environment we can clearly see our students, hear their voices, and touch concrete objects to explain a concept; in the online environment, we need to adapt our senses to connect with learners and create a sense of closeness.

There is also a difference between online and face-to-face classrooms in the ways we interact with our students. The physical environment allows us to easily involve learners in activities and discussions. In the virtual environment, we need to plan these activities intentionally. In the face-to-face environment, we can plan to make changes at the last minute. However, in the online environment, we need to plan well ahead of time; otherwise learners can become confused and frustrated with the lack of direction and guidance. The teaching effort in the face-to-face classroom involves knowing the amount of time needed to focus the mind and emotions, whereas in the online environment, we may feel that we are always connected (Conceição & Lehman, 2011). Table 2.1 summarizes the factors discussed in this chapter that distinguish the face-to-face and online environments.

As you can see in Table 2.1, the two environments require different ways of thinking about designing instruction. The distinguishing factors mean that

Table 2.1. Factors Distinguishing Face-to-Face and Online Environments

Distinguishing Factors	Face-to-Face Environment	Online Environment
Space	Instructor in same space as learners	Learning environment is in an elusive virtual space
Time	There is a clear sense of time	Concept of time is flexible
Boundaries	Instructor in room with learners	There are no geographical limits among instructor and learners
Use of senses	Instructor in close proximity to learners	Due to separate locations, there is a need to adapt senses
Level of interaction	Instructor can easily involve learners	Instructor needs to intentionally develop and implement interactions
Level of planning	Instructor can make last-minute changes	Instructor needs to plan ahead of time
Teaching effort	Focus time for class activities is known	There is a feeling of being constantly connected

course intention, anticipation, prioritization, and envisioning need to be considered in a different way for online courses. Pre-planning takes a different length of time that spans from before the course begins to the end of the course period (Conceição, 2006). Anticipating and prioritizing course activities include looking at the "big picture" when creating the syllabus, predicting the course's timeline, determining activities relevant to the course, defining clear expectations, organizing information in a way that is clear and easy to follow, creating interactions, and making sure the course has a consistent look and feel in the virtual environment. This chapter presents the design strategies that instructors in our study used to retain their online students. Before we present these design strategies, we will address the concept of intentional design.

INTENTIONAL DESIGN FOR ONLINE COURSES

Intentional design is a method that involves purposeful actions and takes into consideration the online learning environment, the teaching process, and learner characteristics. We have noticed in our years of consulting with instructors and conducting research that perceptions about online learning and teaching vary depending on the content, learners, and technology (Lehman & Conceição, 2010; Conceição & Donohue, 2012).

The discipline drives the content and format of the learning experience. For example, if you are teaching a history course, the content focus will dictate the way you teach the course. If your course is content-based, you will address facts, timelines, resources, and people in history. You may expect your learners to recall, understand, apply, analyze, synthesize, and evaluate content by using podcasts of your lecture, engaging students in the discussion forum, conducting quizzes, and requiring students to write short essays. Your role in this history course can be one of lecturer, facilitator, and evaluator.

If you are teaching a nursing course that requires students to learn a skill and apply it in real life, your instruction would most likely be designed very differently. Because this type of course requires skill application, you need to focus the course on the process of acquiring the skills. For example, to learn cardiopulmonary resuscitation (CPR), students would need to simulate reviving a person using specific steps. To evaluate the students, you would need students to account for each step in the procedure. To accomplish this, students could video themselves and upload the video to the learning management system. Your role as the instructor would be to analyze the video and ensure that the procedure was successfully completed.

If your course is in the sciences, you may need to focus the course on both content and process. For example, you might need to require students to learn specific content and apply it in a lab situation. We have seen this happen in a chemistry class, when students participated in a wet lab from home, reflected on the process, and then shared their findings with their classmates and instructor on the class discussion board or using Skype (Conceição & Lehman, 2011). Your role as the instructor would be to monitor the process and evaluate student content learning.

The examples just mentioned demonstrate that the content design needs to be developed differently depending on the discipline and the desired outcomes of a specific course. This process requires intention, anticipation, prioritization, and envisioning. Based on our study, no matter what discipline was being taught, students wanted courses to be relevant and challenging, have real-world application, apply to students' individual interests, and directly relate to students' work. Therefore, instructors in our study realized that they needed to be open to their students' interests. To accomplish this, they used course design elements and strategies that were more likely to help students stay motivated during their online courses.

DESIGN ELEMENTS AND STRATEGIES TO HELP STUDENTS STAY MOTIVATED ONLINE

Instructors who participated in our study recognized intentional course design elements for keeping students motivated in their online courses. For these instructors, the design elements required preplanning and involved: (1) creating the learning environment, (2) planning for the teaching process, and (3) predicting learners' needs. Within each of these design elements, instructors shared strategies for helping students stay motivated in their online courses.

Creating the Learning Environment

In our study, the creation of the learning environment involved the course structure, which played an important role in the intentional design of the online courses. Instructors identified consistency, variety, relevance, and content prioritization as essential course attributes for a successful online experience for students. These attributes provided the instructors with criteria for efficiently and effectively designing the online course environment.

Consistency   For instructors in our study, consistency involved how course information was displayed and the regularity with which the information was presented. Consistency provided flow for the instructors' courses and made it easier for students to create a mental image of what to expect from the courses. One instructor said, "I use a regular routine of introduction, reading, discussion, assignments, feedback, [and then] repeat" for the period of each module or unit, to help students form a clear image in their minds of what is going to happen.

One strategy to create consistency and flow that was shared by a few instructors in our study was to e-mail students reminders and updates weekly. As one instructor commented, "I e-mail reminders for assignments or posts twice a week in addition to course announcements on [the learning management system]." Another strategy was to send an announcement when grades were posted in the learning management system, including rubrics and detailed feedback. These strategies for maintaining consistency and flow were connected to deadlines to provide students with structure and help them manage course workloads.

Variety   In addition to consistency, instructors in our study also considered variety as an attribute. Variety meant including a mix of content (fact-based, process-based, or both), formats (self-paced, group-based, or both), activities (for example, role play, discussions, concept maps, team projects, and labs), and technologies (synchronous, asynchronous, or both) when designing a course. The course could also be designed with a variety of media, such as audio, video, social networking, gaming, blogging, instant messaging, and so on. Instructors stated that variety helped them engage and motivate students in discussion topics and real-time chat sessions and encouraged spontaneous interaction and participation.

One strategy the instructors used when designing a course was to offer choices in what students could do for their assignments. As one instructor said, "I provide variety in the assignments and as much personal choice as possible."

In this case, students could select the topic to develop a project, choose a scenario for solving a problem, or focus a paper on a topic of their interest.

According to the instructors in our study, instructional strategies planned for a course could have an influence on student motivation. Instructors stated that students were more enthusiastic and engaged in the course if these strategies were varied. Instructors used strategies that involved outside classroom assignments and included case examples that connected to news articles, the latest statistics, and popular culture. Using a variety of learning and doing strategies encouraged students' creativity and hands-on experience with concepts. Directly linking to students' issues, questions, and concerns while remaining flexible, based on students' needs, helped engage students with the content.

Technology also had an impact on how students interacted with content and became interested and motivated to learn. Some instructors in our study created videos that brought textbook content to life. As one instructor stated, "[I used] videos that bring textbook content to life (for [the] section on marriage customs, I include short [3- to 4-minute] videos that show cultures that practice polygyny, polyandry, and 'free love')."

Another example of using technology to motivate students to content was to develop podcasts of guest experts in the field and then direct students to the discussion to compare and contrast guest speakers' perspectives. One student explained how he best learned in those situations as the instructor used a variety of strategies: "I learn best when there is supporting material from the professor such as a podcast, voice over PowerPoint, or radio blog of the lecture."

Relevance Another design attribute that emerged from our study was relevance, when course content was pertinent and applicable to students' lives. Instructors stated that students identified the content application focus as a relevant component to keep them motivated in their online courses. Making this component part of the intentional design of the course increased the likelihood that students would persist in the course. When the focus of the content was related to career or profession and applied to real-life problems, students became excited about the subject matter. Instructors said that students became more motivated to learn when they found something practical that they could utilize immediately in their jobs, that could assist them to improve their skills, or that could help them move up in their career. Three quotes from students in our study illustrate the need for relevance:

> I always try to apply it to my professional work. I see how it relates and how I can use the newfound knowledge.

> I keep in mind the real-life problems that I am trying to solve and think about how what I am learning applies to them.

> When I find something practical that I can utilize right away at my job, I feel more motivated to learn more to improve my skills and potential in order to move up in my career.

Content had to be appealing and relevant for students to maintain motivation in the course. Several students said that what motivated them was to "find what's interesting about the work [in the course]." Three other students talked about the relevance of the subject matter:

> If the matter is interesting—it isn't difficult to stay motivated.

> If the subject or course is interesting and the instructor is organized and good, that's a good motivator.

> I think cultivating interest in the subject matter is more important.

For example, when a course was fact-based, instructors could organize the course around a historical timeline, which could include facts or chronological periods. In this case, the intentional structure of the course and flow of information connected learners to past and present experiences and made the course come alive for them.

Another example of relevance from an instructor in our study was a law course in which the instructor referenced current events such as scenarios through which students could use the concepts and information they were learning and identify issues not yet addressed in the course. In a course on human communication and technology, the instructor used current events to "provide a springboard for keeping students' attention on the most contemporary developments." The subject matter itself became the motivator for the students. In both cases, the content tied into students' full-time jobs and was relevant, challenging, and practical to their lives.

One way instructors made current events relevant was to send out weekly announcements that included a question to stimulate a conversation on a specific historical topic. Another example was to select a keyword for a module and start a free-flowing discussion of the module content. A link in the announcement area directed students to the discussion board for a talk that then led to a more in-depth, highly focused conversation about the subject.

Content Prioritization   The last course attribute identified by instructors in our study was content prioritization. Prioritizing the course content involved organizing the sequence and time of the materials. By using the chunking technique, some instructors in our study divided the course content into small pieces called "chunks" and strategically arranged the materials into modules or units to make reading and understanding more efficient and effective for their students. Two instructors explained well the reasons why they used the chunking technique:

> [I have] many small assignments. [I use] "chunking" of material . . . presenting the material in a highly organized [way], same things always in same order [to reduce] mental overload so [students] can focus on the content.

> [I use] "chunking" content so that students can feel a sense of completion regarding each module.

The chunking technique in these two cases helped the students reduce cognitive overload and allowed them to focus on the content without becoming overwhelmed. In addition, students felt that setting deadlines helped them prioritize content and anticipate what was going to happen during the course period. Three students concurred with the need for having deadlines:

> Deadlines are what keep me motivated. I have a lot of things to split my time on, so I have to figure out what is due first and go from there.

> I use deadlines . . . to keep track of when assignments are due or when I need to post by to determine what I do first.

> [I need to] make sure [I] know deadlines every week and set aside time to complete the task at least a day in advance; if any difficulties arise, they can be handled.

These quotes show that chunking content and setting up deadlines assisted students in prioritizing information. Certain courses had self-paced activities with deadlines in which students could decide when to work on a task and when to complete it. Some of the instructors in our study used a checklist with due dates for students to accomplish tasks within a course. Having this checklist available gave students the flexibility to log in to the course multiple times per week at their own pace, mark what they had completed, and meet the course deadlines.

According to the instructors in our study, setting regular deadlines and milestones for modules or units was another way for them to keep their students motivated and engaged regularly. This provided a sense of control for both the instructor and students, who could then better decide how to manage tasks based on content delivery. One instructor stated how she set the regular deadlines and milestones: "I try to maintain a regular schedule of work and study." Based on our study findings, prioritizing by chunking content and setting up deadlines had an impact on how students persisted in the online courses.

Planning for the Teaching Process

Because the online environment is elusive, it can easily go unobserved. Therefore, there was a need for instructors in our study to create a vision of the environment in their minds, feel it, and act upon it in order to become part of it with their students. To make the online environment real, instructors used intentional design when planning for the teaching process. Intentional design for teaching included setting up clear expectations, personalizing the environment through interactions, and incorporating feedback throughout the course.

Setting Up Clear Expectations   In our study, a recurring theme from the instructors was the need for making things well-defined from the beginning of the course by setting up clear expectations and guidelines for students. This involved identifying well-established course goals, module or unit objectives, and course outcomes; assignments and tasks to accomplish during the course; and deadlines. Two instructors emphasized the importance of setting up expectations from the beginning of the course:

> I [lay out] the assignments, expectations, and deadlines from the beginning to allow the student[s] to work these in [their schedule].

> [I] clearly note expectations from the start. Course organization is clear [and] everything is set up for the semester when the student accesses the course for the first time.

Expectations also had to be realistic and relevant for the students because they needed to be prepared for the semester. One student said that it was essential to have "a comprehensive syllabus where expectations and assignments are made crystal clear—no guessing!" Another student stated, "Before the course begins, I access the syllabus and identify expectations and learning outcomes." "Clearly stated expectations by [the] instructor of how much and what kind of participation is required" were also indispensable for student success, as another student said.

For instructors, the first step in designing the online course was to create the syllabus, which included defining overall goals for the course (the "big picture"), module or unit objectives ("small chunks" within a course), and student outcomes (what students were expected to do after completing the course). Goals, objectives, and outcomes had to be aligned with each other. The expectations for these three components of the course had to be consistent, relevant, and realistic for the students to feel as though they were part of something that was real.

Next, the course assignments and tasks had to be defined and strategically arranged to align with goals and objectives without overwhelming students. One instructor said that "clear tasks [and] strategic arrangement of course material [facilitated] accomplishing goals without being overburdening or mystical." A course with detailed instructions and well-established deadlines gave students a sense of organization and time, pace of the experience, and a feeling of control over their learning process. These all contributed to helping students stay motivated and persist in the online courses.

Personalizing the Online Environment Through Interactions Another way instructors in our study made the elusive online environment more tangible was through personalizing interactions. Including interactions was necessary whether the course was self-paced or group-based. In a self-paced course, interactions happened with the content and the instructor. Personalizing content interactions meant creating a warm feeling of presence and a conversational tone when developing materials in text, graphic, audio, or video formats. In group-based courses, interactions were developed and planned in a different way. Here, the core of the planning was creating presence between instructor and students and among students with a sense of community and trust. Presence required participants' openness to different perspectives, shared leadership, cooperation, collaboration, mutual support, responsiveness, and active engagement. Examples of how instructors personalized the online environment through interactions follow:

> I personalize my contributions to the discussions that recognize strengths in individuals' contributions to discussion threads. I invite students to arrange phone meetings with me.
>
> [I] provide personalized feedback to all students before they even have to ask for help.
>
> [I use] e-mail [in] a somewhat personal nature, for example, acknowledging the shared experience of pursuing a degree while parenting.

Because of the lack of a set space and time to interact with others online, there was a sense of omnipresence, but this did not have to be the case. Setting deadlines and making oneself known in the online environment at specific times, by personalizing the experience, helped avoid the feeling that instructors and students were always there. In this situation, deadlines helped set boundaries. Personalizing created a feeling of closeness and availability.

To build a stronger sense of online community, instructors made themselves available through synchronous meetings early in the course. One instructor said, "Voice contact via telephone is highly motivating, particularly for nontraditional students." Synchronous meetings involved weekly virtual office hours that provided the opportunity for the students to be heard and to connect with the instructor to discuss class materials. These meetings, which were held using Skype and other synchronous environments, created a personal atmosphere. During these hours, instructors provided clarification of class assignments, student encouragement and support, demonstrations, and tutoring or mentoring.

Another strategy for personalizing through interactions was to enable students to share leadership during discussion. As one instructor stated, "I put students in charge of organizing and moderating discussion. They want to appear organized and intelligent to their peers (I assume), so are motivated to do well here." Sharing leadership allowed students to feel in control over the process, gave them a sense of contributing to the team, and motivated them to accomplish tasks.

A strategy shared by one instructor to personalize the online classroom was the use of announcements. As this instructor stated, "I e-mail [students] weekly with updates, announcements, or reminders, and I keep things in 'bite sized' pieces." These announcements created presence, enhanced personalization, conveyed enthusiasm, and gave students a feeling of support.

Incorporating Feedback Throughout the Course In our study, instructors used feedback as an assessment of a process, a product, or a student's performance on a task; this feedback was used as a basis for improvement. Including feedback as part of the intentional design of the online course was a strategy that motivated students and encouraged them to persist in the course. Feedback was individual or group, provided at different times during the period of the course, and used for different purposes (performance improvement or team assessment).

Individual feedback was provided via e-mail, through the grading area of the learning management system, or during synchronous sessions. Group feedback was provided via general announcements, in the group discussion board, or in the team discussion area. The frequency of feedback was very important for the instructors in our study because the feedback gave formative and summative assessment of how the student was performing in the course. Instructors stated that the time and frequency (regularly, consistently, and promptly) of feedback kept students motivated during the course.

For instructors in our study, regular feedback meant providing feedback on an ongoing basis throughout the course and involved recognition of student work, as these quotes illustrate:

> [I provide] ongoing positive feedback; recognition for insightful learning; and modules that offer a "routine" meaning. [Feedback] looks similar from week to week.

> [I] provide ongoing feedback [and] additional resources.

> My students are supported in developing their analysis of texts and in working through course concepts via group discussion and feedback, as well as with regular writing assignments and feedback [that I provide].

> [I use] weekly feedback, open forum for questions that I or peers can respond to, and regular posts to the news wall to answer common questions.

[I use] daily (except Sunday) feedback in discussion groups, online chats, and e-mail.

[I e-mail] students who are not online or posting regularly. [I use] follow-up phone conferences with students after feedback on papers.

Consistent feedback made students feel self-confident and provided them with a consistent pace, as these instructors explained:

[My] students are provided with a recommended schedule, study guides, and personalized feedback on the content they [do not understand] fully.

[I] incorporate feedback among students as a part of graded assignments.

[I] use similar language each week.

Prompt feedback had to do with response time and how the instructors followed up on questions, assignments, and students' performance, as these quotes show:

[I provide] detailed feedback on individual and team assignments . . . timely follow-up.

[I use] 24 [hour] turnaround with questions except on weekends, [and provide] feedback at the end of each module.

I provide feedback no more than 24 [hours] later, and they can submit again—this iteration can occur several times if necessary.

[I provide] timely replies to student e-mails.

[My] support is [given] largely through both group and individual feedback, and fast response to student questions that are posted to a discussion board.

Students in our study provided their own perspectives on the impact of feedback on their motivation. For example, when students received regular, consistent, and prompt feedback, they felt it strengthened their learning and directed their understanding. As one student stated, "I look forward to reading feedback after I post in a discussion from the instructor. This either solidifies or guides understanding of the course concepts." When the instructor was present in the course, students had positive feelings about the instructor and felt motivated about the course. As one student said about the instructor's participation in the discussion,

"The instructor is knowledgeable and an active participant offering feedback and prompting inquiry."

The type and format of feedback had an effect on students' performance. Instructors in our study shared ways in which they provided feedback. They used praise, encouragement, recognition for insightful learning, constructive criticism, and rewards. Praise and encouragement provided positive reinforcement for students to build their confidence and persist in the course. Recognizing students' progress in an open forum or individually from module to module helped students become aware of their learning growth. Constructive criticism based on a rubric showed students how their work improved or expanded upon content and kept them motivated to do better.

Constructive criticism was not always received well by everyone and could have a negative impact on students' performance and self-esteem. Instructors said that it was important to consider the language when providing constructive criticism by using a positive tone. They also said that rewards for going above and beyond assigned work were supplied through bonus points, extra credit, or assignment waiver.

Predicting Learners' Needs

Another area of the online intentional course design that was instrumental in retaining students and helping them persist in the course, for the instructors in our study, was predicting learners' needs. This meant identifying students' needs, foreseeing challenges students had in participating in the course, and preempting problems that could occur. Instructors identified students' needs as skill deficiencies related to the course, lack of academic preparation for an online course, and inability to access resources.

These learners' needs could create challenges for students to be successful online. Instructors in our study used orientation activities and open forums as strategies to preempt anticipated problems. Three instructors explained how they developed orientation activities and what they included:

> I have an "orientation" PowerPoint for the first lecture separate from any content that goes [with] the syllabus and sets up expectations for the semester. I provide a discussion forum that is open throughout the semester for only questions related to administration of the course (no course content).

> [I provide] extremely detailed orientation documents, discussion forums dedicated to asking questions, allowing students to help each other.

> [I use an] orientation at the beginning [of the course] (getting to know the other students), a mix of individual, small group, and large group work, messages via e-mail or course home page at the beginning and end of every week.

In addition to a student orientation in the beginning of the course, instructors in our study also incorporated tutorials, lists of frequently asked questions (FAQs), and ongoing help discussion forums to assist students. These strategies eliminated emotional disruption and provided a more receptive atmosphere for learning.

In our study, instructors also anticipated students' needs by making available campus support resources through course links or reminders throughout the course, as these quotes indicate:

> I try to repeat information related to student support (online tutoring, Help Desk, IT support, etc.) frequently throughout the course.

> I constantly ask the students if I can help them. I work with the office of disabilities to understand what students need so I can support them.

> E-mail is [my] primary way [for students] to get the support from me. I [also] have virtual office hours in which I can meet with students.

Predicting learners' needs appeared to be a time saver for the instructors in our study because it helped them anticipate issues before they surfaced. Students who are new to the online environment can be easily overwhelmed by the layout of a course. That is when the concepts of "big picture" and "small chunks," as mentioned by the instructors in our study, could be part of the intentional design of the course to meet learners' needs. These concepts are applicable even with experienced learners, as each course may present a different layout.

Although the instructors in our study did not mention following a specific instructional design model to plan and implement online courses, their stories included the essential elements of any instructional design approach. Through course attributes (consistency, variety, relevance, and content prioritization), instructors established a set of criteria to meet their students' motivational needs. The set of criteria was integrated into their teaching process and had an impact on the intentional design of their courses.

THE IMPACT OF INTENTIONAL DESIGN FOR ONLINE COURSE SUCCESS

The instructors who participated in our study used purposeful actions to design their online courses that took into consideration the online learning environment, the teaching process, and learner characteristics. The design of the online learning environment included a course structure with a set of criteria that helped students stay motivated during the course. Course structure was about more than simply making sure that a course was well organized; the structure of the course had to help the student create a reliable mental image of the course without distractions. In our experience, we have seen students lose focus in courses that present too much information and lack consistent structure.

Often instructors create courses without a full understanding of what it means to be an online learner. A recent study by Terantino and Agbehonou (2012) shows the importance of instructor perceptions when they become online learners in a faculty development program. By participating in this program, instructors were able to see the relevance of certain strategies when preparing their own courses.

Faculty development websites and blogs address the significance of chunking information and materials for the online learning environment. In our study, chunking occurred during content prioritization, course announcements, and student feedback. For us, establishing the course structure starts with chunking during the design of the online environment. Structuring the course continues during the teaching process through communicating and interacting with students, creating a sense of presence, and providing support. Communicating and interacting with students in a consistent manner lets students know what to expect. Creating presence personalizes the experience and helps students feel connected. Providing instructional support through psychological and emotional assistance via interactions and feedback can help create and maintain presence without distraction. Providing technical support through detailed documents about the course, answers to FAQs, and help forums can alleviate frustration and reduce anxiety (Lehman & Conceição, 2010).

By taking into consideration the online learning environment and the teaching process, instructors can interrelate the instructional components and better meet learners' needs. This is part of a dynamic process. In this process, the instructor must be aware of the "big picture" of the course and at the same time intentionally address the small details that make the elusive course feel real.

An example from our own research of how intentional design impacts the success of an online program is the case of the Erikson Online degree program in early childhood education (Conceição & Donohue, 2012). This case study on students' perceptions of their online learning experience and the effects of that experience on student learning shows the impact of intentional design in this online program. One important aspect of the Erikson Online degree program is the way it responds to the learners' general characteristics: learners had inadequate technology skills and limited online experiences and were full-time workers. The instructional design team intentionally built the program courses to meet learners' needs, keeping in mind the motto "easy to access, simple to use, and impossible to get lost." The program design is based on creating a sense of presence through community building and support.

The impact of intentional design in the Erikson Online degree program, based on the learners' characteristics as well as the online environment and the teaching process, is the outcome of:

- an organized learning environment that provides relevant, consistent, practical, and timely materials to help students connect to their professional practice;
- the use of technologies to create presence;
- a supportive staff team that provides professional, sensible, and efficient assistance;
- a team of instructors who design learner-centered instruction and encourage students to gain confidence, become independent, and apply knowledge to their specific professional needs;
- the use of teaching methods that encourage interaction, establish presence, and motivate students to participate in an in-depth, convenient, and flexible environment in which they have control over their learning process; and
- the use of online community building strategies that foster involvement and engagement in the learning process (Conceição & Donohue, 2012).

Although we do not have data about the relationship between intentional design and student retention, there was a clear relationship between intentional design and student satisfaction (Conceição & Donohue, 2012). This program uses a cohort model, which can make it easier to monitor learner readiness for online learning and the use of technology. In this case, retention could have been influenced by the characteristics of the students in a given cohort and could have impacted the intentional design of the course. More studies are needed to clarify the relationship between intentional design and student retention.

DESIGN STRATEGIES FOR RETAINING ONLINE STUDENTS

This chapter presented the factors distinguishing the face-to-face and online learning environments, intentional design for online courses, and course design elements and strategies to help students stay motivated online. Online teaching requires intentional design and pre-planning, including (1) creating the learning environment in a specific way with certain features in mind, (2) planning for the teaching process with certain design elements and strategies, and (3) predicting learners' needs with strategies that anticipate and preempt problems. Table 2.2 provides a summary of course design elements, strategies, and ways to integrate the strategies into course design.

Creating the online environment with intentional design allows us, as instructors, to anticipate, prioritize, and envision the whole course from a "big picture" perspective prior to the beginning of the course. Once the course is designed and ready to be implemented, we can focus on the process of the course. During course implementation, the process allows for creating a sense of presence through interactions with students, monitoring student progress, and assessing student performance. The course process not only helps us focus primarily on the learner, but also helps us manage our workload.

The way in which the instructor designs the online course determines the way students schedule time and tasks, develop study skills, and are motivated to learn. The next chapter will focus on student strategies for staying motivated online. These strategies are based on a pathway for students and include self-awareness, self-efficacy, purpose or goals, the means to achieve the goals, and rewards for achieving goals. Chapter 3 also provides an explanation of our study findings from a motivational perspective and concludes with a discussion of how to incorporate motivating strategies into course design.

Table 2.2. Course Design Elements, Strategies, and Ways to Integrate the Strategies into Course Design

Course Design Element	Strategy	Ways to Integrate Strategy Into Course Design
Learning Environment	Being consistent	Present information in a consistent way for content, readings, assignments, and feedback
	Using variety	E-mail reminders and updates weekly
	Being relevant	Send announcements when grades are posted
	Prioritizing content	Use different media (audio, video, social networking, gaming, blogging, instant messaging, etc.) to engage students in discussion topics and encourage spontaneous interaction and participation
		Give students choices in learning based on variety of assignments
		Include various case examples that connect to news articles, latest statistics, and popular culture
		Use a variety of learning and doing activities that encourage creativity and hands-on experiences
		Present content in different formats using technology to bring textbook content to life, for example, podcasts of guest experts
		Present and connect content related to career, profession, or real-life problems
		Connect learners to past and present experiences based on a chronological timeline
		Send out a weekly announcement with a current event question to start a conversation on a specific topic in the discussion area

Continued

Table 2.2. Continued

Course Design Element	Strategy	Ways to Integrate Strategy Into Course Design
		Select a keyword for a module related to skills being learned and start a free-flowing discussion of the module content
		Use the chunking technique to divide course content into small pieces and strategically arrange materials into modules or units to make reading and understanding more efficient and effective
		Set deadlines for students to prioritize information and anticipate course activities
		Include self-paced activities with deadlines for students to decide when to work on a task and when to complete it
		Use a checklist with due dates to give students flexibility and control over their tasks
		Set regular deadlines and milestones for modules or units to keep students motivated and engaged
Teaching Process	Setting up clear expectations	Develop the course syllabus to include the course goals, module or unit objectives, and course outcomes; assignments and tasks to accomplish during the course; and deadlines
		Strategically arrange course assignments to align with goals and objectives without overwhelming students
	Personalizing online environment through interactions	Create a warm feeling of presence and a conversational tone when developing written, audio, or video materials
		Recognize individuals' strengths and contributions to discussion threads
	Incorporating feedback throughout the course	Provide personalized feedback to each student
		Acknowledge individual student's leadership via e-mail when it is unique
		Schedule synchronous meetings with students early in the course to clarify assignments and check on student online comfort

	Schedule virtual office hours weekly to clarify assignments, deal with issues and preempt problems, demonstrate a skill, tutor, or mentor students
	Share leadership with students during course discussion to allow students to feel in control over their learning process, create a sense of community, and gain self-confidence
	Send out weekly announcements that have a personal tone
	Give prompt individual feedback through the learning management system grading area and inform students you have done this via e-mail
	Provide team project feedback via the team discussion area in the learning management system or e-mail the feedback to all team members
	Include personal feedback for individual writing assignments
	Have a phone conversation with a student as a follow-up to an assignment feedback when necessary
	Use a rubric to grade assignments and recognize individual or group progress
	Consider the language and tone when providing positive and constructive criticism in your comments to students
Learners' Needs	
Planning for students' lack of academic preparation and creating student readiness for online courses	Provide detailed orientation documents
	Use PowerPoint to go over the syllabus and to help set up expectations
	Include tutorials and FAQs as part of the orientation activities to prepare students for the course
	Use help forums for students to ask questions of each other or exchange information
	Have an open discussion forum available for non-content-related course administration questions
Identifying students' skill deficiencies or special needs to preempt problems before they occur	Encourage students to seek remedial centers for writing, math, and so on
	Work with the office of disabilities to support students with special needs
Assuring that all course resources are accessible	Incorporate links of campus resources into the learning management system for easy access

Student Strategies for Staying Motivated Online

The previous chapter focused on course design strategies for retaining online students. In this chapter, we look at strategies identified by students for staying motivated in online courses and the pathway for students to follow that emerged from our analysis of the findings of our study. By understanding this pathway, instructors can better meet students' needs and use approaches that influence student motivation to learn. Based on our study findings, student strategies were considered essential for successful completion of online courses. This chapter presents the pathway that students in our study followed and the strategies they used to stay motivated when learning online. Next, the chapter explains study findings from a motivational perspective and concludes with how to incorporate motivating strategies into the course design.

PATHWAY AND STRATEGIES FOR STAYING MOTIVATED IN ONLINE COURSES

In our study, students identified strategies that kept them motivated when taking online courses. When analyzed, the strategies showed a consistent pattern of a pathway for students. The strategies involved self-awareness, self-efficacy (self-value), a purpose or goals, the means to achieve the goal or goals, and rewards for achieving the goal or goals.

Self-Awareness

In our study, students who viewed themselves as motivated were self-aware and able to clearly identify strategies that they believed made their online learning experience successful. One of the study participants said, "I'm [. . .] a self-disciplined person and have no problem staying ahead on my work because I don't want to fall behind." This statement indicates that this person is self-aware, knows the learning process, understands the situation, and recognizes the consequences of not moving on efficiently.

In our experience, it is during course orientation activities that students have a chance to become more aware of what it means to be an online learner, to understand the online environment, and to recognize what is necessary to succeed in the course. Some of the strategies we use in our courses include pre-course surveys of technology skills and content knowledge. We also provide an opportunity for students to learn about one another and feel that they are not alone in their learning journey. We use icebreakers related to the course content. For example, in an instructional design and teaching strategies course, where students go through an instructional design process to create a course, they are asked to share a teaching biography.

In another course, where the main assignment is to design an online course, students prepare an introductory biographical slide with their pictures and narratives of their previous online learning experience. Each individual slide would then become part of the class introductory album. This album not only creates self-awareness and a sense of online group presence but also lays a foundation for trust. When online students learn about other students in the course and begin to feel a sense of trust, it is more likely they will have a positive attitude about the learning experience.

Becoming aware of the process of learning in the online environment required time and experience for study participants. Students in our study who had taken one or two courses online had different experiences from students who had taken more than three courses online. Each course might be designed by instructors using different formats, interactive strategies, and technologies. The role of the instructor can also determine the overall experience for the student. As a result, students may have to adapt to each online learning experience. The more experience students have, the more likely they are to be open and self-aware of the online environment. Over time, based on a series of experiences, students develop strategies that help them become successful and persist in the online course. These strategies can be affected by students' self-efficacy and level of motivation.

Self-Efficacy

In our study findings, self-efficacy emerged as the conviction of one's value and capability to organize and put into action what was necessary to successfully move ahead and complete an online course. Self-efficacy was determined by how people thought, felt, and behaved in the online environment. Motivation was the reason (the cognitive state) for the desire (the psychological state) to accomplish something (the behavioral state). One participant described her strategies to stay motivated in accomplishing the online coursework through this quote:

> As a nontraditional student, my main motivating factors are self-determination [cognitive] and positive thinking [psychological]. Before the course begins, I access the syllabus and identify expectations and learning outcomes. If possible I start working on assignments ahead of time [behavioral]. I try not to allow my assignments [to] pile up on me [psychological]. To keep up with group discussions, I check in anytime I am in front of a computer [behavioral], I don't have to respond each of these times if I need more time to process my thoughts [cognitive].

In this quote, self-efficacy is the student's belief to put into action the goals to complete the online course. The student uses self-determination and positive thinking as the reason and desire to complete the course and then lays out the strategies to accomplish that goal: access the syllabus, identify expectations and learning outcomes, start working on assignments, and so on. This example shows that this student had experience taking online courses and had a plan. Self-efficacy and motivation played an important role in this student's perceptions.

In our online courses, when students are new to the online environment, we make sure they are ready for the learning experience by having them work through a scavenger hunt. During this activity, students navigate the different areas of the learning management system to become familiar with the structure of the course and gain a sense of control over the learning environment. It is important for instructors to monitor student progress through the learning analytics in the learning management system throughout the course. The learning analytics take the form of statistical reports of student access and use of the different course areas. When we find that students are not actively participating, we set up one-on-one meetings to discuss why they are not participating and then we identify strategies to help them become successful in the course. Often, the reason that students are not active participants in the course is their lack of awareness, self-confidence, conviction, and belief that they are able to move forward.

A Purpose for Taking a Course

In our study, students explained that to keep them motivated in completing online coursework they needed to have a purpose or a goal or goals. Students used strategies to achieve a goal or small goals throughout the online course. As the goal or small goals were achieved, these students gained rewards or rewarded themselves.

Having a purpose or a goal of completion was an intrinsic incentive for students in our study that kept them motivated to complete a course. Either they set one specific goal or they set small goals throughout the course. Some reasons that kept them motivated to accomplish a specific goal were having an end in sight such as obtaining a degree, taking a course to complete the major requirements, and doing well in the course. Several students said that their main goal was to finish their degree and get it over with. A few students said that they were motivated to take a course because it was a necessary class to complete their major. Others felt that they wanted to do well in a course because they were paying for it and didn't want to waste money, as these students stated:

> The money to pay for the course seems more out-of-pocket than for regular courses so I want to do well so as not to feel like I wasted money.

> It costs more so I don't want to waste the extra money. I go at my own pace so I should have no problems keeping up since I don't have to go to campus for online classes.

Some students felt that setting small goals during the course motivated them to persist. These small goals could be about accomplishing specific tasks. Two students explained what it meant for them in detail:

> I want to get x done by this day, etc. Also, knowing what my graduate degree can get me in terms of jobs, thinking about the confidence booster finishing will bring.

> I set a goal for myself to complete before stopping (e.g., study for and take two quizzes).

No matter how big or small the goals were, having a sense of accomplishment motivated the students to achieve a purpose. This purpose was achieved through specific means that helped them work toward the goal. Sometimes we have students who register for a course without a specific purpose or goal. By asking students to complete an individual data form that asks about their course goals, we can find out whether our course is a good fit for the student. This form should be completed in the beginning of the course, so that students can figure out whether the course is worth their time and money.

Means to Achieve Goals

Based on the themes that emerged from our study, the means students used to achieve a goal or goals involved three strategies: time management, prioritizing, and learning. The term *strategies* here refers to recurring patterns of coping with new information, issues, and behaviors. Time management strategies comprise the methods and skills students used to achieve their goals and effectively and efficiently accomplish course tasks. Prioritizing strategies involved identifying tasks and ranking them in order of importance. Learning strategies were methods for learning content and procedures that influenced students' study habits.

Time Management Strategies Time management strategies were ones in which students had control over themselves, their time, and their pace. Self-control involved students' restricting actions, forcing accomplishments, and reminding themselves about task completion. One student said, "I edit the host's file on my computer and time lock it so that I am restricted from visiting websites during my allotted study times." Another student said, "Reminding myself that it's just like a normal class, it needs to get done. Writing it as a part of my to-do list during the week." Some students forced themselves to do the homework, to be on task, and get the modules done for the course. One student even said that "scheduling time and keeping hydrated" were important to stay motivated.

Self-control over time involved structure, flexibility, and convenience for when to accomplish tasks. Having a structured time to accomplish tasks was a way to avoid becoming overwhelmed. Students structured their time by conducting online work every day, having a "rigid" structure such as working nightly, staying on schedule with reading and posting assignments, keeping up on the work, having to set due dates, and setting aside a specific time as if it were a class time.

One student said, "I usually do much in the early a.m. when I feel fresh and creative." Another said that "reading before online discussions and doing work on time" were all strategies that helped maintain control over time. Online learning is not only convenient but also flexible. One student explained, "Knowing I can check it off my to-do list when it's convenient for me was helpful." Another stated, "I usually like the flexibility of being able to finish before the deadline, it gives me a feeling of accomplishment and finishing a task before a deadline."

Another area of self-control that students identified was having control over the pace of their lives. The term *pace* in this case means having a rhythm for accomplishing tasks as if they were taking face-to-face courses. This rhythm was marked by the course deadlines. The flow of the rhythm varied from one individual to another depending on the condition. For some students, pressure motivated them to accomplish a task. As one student said, "I just pace myself. Sometimes, I long for the pressure of turning in an assignment by the deadline so I will push it to the last minute." For other students, a steady pace allowed for sufficient time. Some students set their own pace by working a little bit every day, setting aside certain days and times to get reading done, and obtaining materials early so they could start ahead of time. By setting aside time for class, students could better self-manage their time and feel undisturbed and comfortable when they needed to get caught up on the material they were learning. Instead of allowing the course to manage their lives, these students took control and self-managed their pace for the course.

Students managed their time when taking an online course by setting a schedule based on deadlines and life roles and tasks.

Setting a Schedule Based on Deadlines   One method students identified as keeping them motivated when taking an online course was blocking out a specific time for doing the coursework. This time was contingent upon what the instructor required, and students planned accordingly based on their schedules and course deadlines.

Due dates and deadlines set the framework for students to manage their time for the online course. Timelines helped students stay on track. If students were taking more than one course, they could look at the deadlines for both courses and determine when to schedule time to study, complete homework, and participate in discussions. One student stated, "Deadlines are what keep me motivated. I have a lot of things to split my time on so I have to figure out what is due first and go from there."

Students in our study set specific times for reading, contributions to the discussion, and homework based on course deadlines. Also, students blocked out times for each class if more than one class was being taken. Some students made sure to take days off from doing online work either during the week or on the weekend. Other students specified the frequency with which they accessed the course and the set routine they used for managing their time.

For example, for some students days off and evenings were scheduled for reading, working on projects, and so on. Others spent Monday and Tuesday for reading materials, Wednesday through Saturday participating in discussions and working on written assignments, and Sunday as a day off. Another way of blocking out time was setting aside one full day to study, read, take notes, and get caught up on the most recent information; then, throughout the week, study the material just learned. For online contributions, students would set up specific days such as Tuesday, Thursday, or Friday evenings and, depending on the course workload, sometimes on Sundays. For students taking more than one online course, they devoted one to two nights per week per online course to reading course material and then doing homework and quizzes. Another method for students taking more than one online course was for them to set up one two-hour block of time for each class per week and a separate one-hour block of time for the same class later in the week.

Having a predictable schedule was also a way to manage time. Frequency and routine determined their schedule. Some students completed as much as they could during the beginning of the week, so that they had time to review and go over the material several times before getting a head start the following week. Others tried to make time for the online class every day or blocked out a window of time on the weekend to work on the class. One participant in our study said, "I did most of my studies between the hours of 3:00 a.m. and 6:00 a.m. every day. This is when my brain is well relaxed and ready to [absorb] without constant daytime distractions." Others were more rigid in scheduling their time by having a specific day to work on the course and stick to that schedule. One student considered "each course as a regular work schedule" and tried hard to protect that schedule. By protecting their schedules, students ensured that they could complete their work in an effective amount of time. Some made sure that they were always "a week ahead in assignments" so that they would not fall behind.

Having a regularly scheduled time for the course helped the students better manage their time. Checking the course frequently, almost every day, was helpful for some students, while other students set aside time on weekends or late at night, said "to be [their] quiet period and a time when [they] were able to better concentrate." Students who were new to the online environment felt it harder to be in online courses "when the instructor expected [them] to be online and post contributions often rather than more periodically."

Setting a Schedule Based on Life Roles and Tasks   Life roles had an impact on ways in which students managed their time for their online courses. These roles included being a full-time worker, a parent, or a full-time student and defined their schedule. Students scheduled their time based on their obligations and tasks, as explained by the following quotes:

> I do all my schoolwork during the day while my children are at school and my husband is at work, and I work part-time second shift.
>
> I always start homework after I am done making dinner and take a break every two hours.
>
> I usually get readings and such done while at work since I work a desk job anyway, I usually save papers for the weekends.
>
> I work full-time and attend school full-time so having the ability to plan my week around the two makes things easier. Online allows for that.
>
> I work on school when I am not at work . . . and I make time for my family.

For people who had families, their schedules revolved around their families. One student said, "I study during my children's naps, and make arrangements with my spouse to care for the children on certain nights so I can work." In addition to balancing coursework with families, students also took friends into consideration and let family and friends know when they had time for them. Doing so allowed students to remain healthy and manage stress. Because it was easy for students to underestimate the time it would take them to complete assignments to their satisfaction, they tried to maintain a regular schedule of work, study, and family life.

Depending on their learning style, some students preferred to complete one segment at a time, then do some housework, and then do another segment. Another example of a preferable learning environment to focus on the course was when the children were absent. As one student stated, "I engage with online classes solely when my kids are gone and I am able to focus on the content." Others typically did schoolwork for two to four hours, three to four nights a week after their children were in bed.

Prioritizing Strategies   Prioritizing was another means to achieve students' goals. Prioritizing involved identifying tasks and ranking them in order of importance. As one student stated, "[for me] prioritizing and scheduling [are] deciding how much time to devote to each class, each project, and arranging what needs to be done first." In our study, students used specific strategies to prioritize time, documents, tasks, and family affairs. Students used planners, calendars, to-do lists, or organizational charts as tools to map their schedules and tasks. Because the class did not meet face-to-face, students purposefully scheduled time and tasks for the course based on due dates.

One of the study participants shared a method to prioritize time: "I mark all due dates in a planner and write reminders a day or so before something's due." Another way of prioritizing was to highlight important sections to be read at the end of the week. One participant accomplished this by writing important concepts of each week on Dry Erase™ boards, using one board for each class.

Taking online courses is not just a matter of scheduling time but also organizing and prioritizing documents in a consistent way. As one student said, "Online courses require a lot of documents to be produced; therefore, I need to organize data clearly. When saving or submitting documents, I do so in the same manner. . . I include my name, the course, and the assignment." For some students, printing off reading materials and keeping them in a binder and a digital folder helped them prioritize information. Another method students used was "highlighting when major tasks were due and setting a goal start date" so they would not work at the last minute.

Making the elusive world of online learning real helped students to be more successful. To do that, students wrote down when things were due on a calendar and set aside time each day to do the work just as though they were going to a traditional class environment. One student said that she "scheduled time in my planner like an in-person class."

Another way to prioritize time and tasks was suggested by a student in our study who looked for gaps in his schedule and then planned out when to do his online coursework. After discovering the schedule openings, he said:

> I complete my homework at night and prefer when a class doesn't have multiple deadlines in a week, but rather one week-long deadline for various assignments during the week. It's too hard to make my schedule work around due dates that close only a day after they open.

By using deadlines, students kept track of when assignments were due or when they needed to post in the discussion forum. Students usually did whatever took the least amount of time first and then worked from there. For example, many students worked on having a plan prior to the start of each week and staying organized. Depending on the week, students figured out what might be the best day or days to complete that week's assignment or task and then outlined objectives and crossed them off as they completed them.

Another strategy students used to prioritize time and tasks was to create an organizational chart and timeline before the course began to track due dates and assignment requirements. Mapping out the coursework on a calendar kept the students motivated and on track. Also, using the chart assisted them in seeing the course laid out in front of them step by step with clear goals to complete one by one. By doing so, students were able to break up tasks and accomplish them a little every day.

Prioritizing also meant fitting in tasks and assignments as appropriate and staying on pace with readings in whatever free time they had. One student in our study described how this was done:

I try to fit in the readings a little bit everywhere I can, but I usually set aside a specific time to try and get it done (much like scheduling a class), but on my own time. That way it is easy to reschedule if need be.

In contrast to prioritizing and scheduling specific times, some students "played it by ear" or worked on coursework during their free time (during their off time from class and work). For example, one student worked on the course "whenever I have at least three hours to work on stuff and get my head in the game." Another student said:

> Whenever I have time and energy. The best thing about online courses is that you can work whenever it fits into your schedule. The worst thing about online courses is that they are 24/7. I tried to schedule my coursework like a traditional class, by using nights or evenings to do homework and reading, and always tried to schedule completing tasks ahead of time so I was able to take a day or two away from the discussion without feeling guilty.

Prioritizing had different meanings for each individual. For some students, prioritizing meant working consistently on what they were doing. For others, prioritizing could mean fitting in coursework whenever they had time among teaching, other classes, and other assignments; creating a to-do list or a chart; or using a calendar or a planner.

Learning Strategies   In our study, learning strategies were methods for achieving learning goals, objectives, and outcomes. Learning strategies appeared to be linked to the needs and interests of students to enhance their learning. Learning online requires different cognitive and affective efforts from classroom learning. Cognitive effort involves the mental processes students go through when taking online courses. Affective effort involves the psychological and emotional processes students go through to make the virtual feel real. These efforts require students to adapt their thinking and senses to the online environment.

To adapt to the online environment, students in our study used different strategies from what they would use in the face-to-face classroom to organize, convey, and relate information and interact with others. Students used certain learning strategies to accommodate these differences when learning content and procedures at different levels. We used Svinicki's (2004) Instructional Pathway to Self-Regulation Model to identify the learning strategies students in our study used. The model uses the acronym *GAMES*, which stands for the following:

- Goal-oriented study, which requires the ability to set goals and bring together resources to achieve goals. Goal-oriented study involves planning before studying—for example, previewing the course material and the problem set and laying out key questions based on the preview. Students who know what they want to accomplish have a better chance of achieving it.

- Active studying, which involves the ability to engage in active processing of the material—for instance, paraphrasing or creating one's own examples. Students who can involve their minds as well as their senses are engaged in active studying.

- Meaning and memorable studying, which requires the ability to relate to prior knowledge and interests. This kind of studying involves creating one's own examples, making connections across courses and modules, and expanding on concept details.

- Explaining the materials in order to learn, which involves the ability to explain learned material in one's own words to someone else.

- Self-monitoring, which requires the ability to monitor understanding and make corrections. Self-monitoring can be accomplished by comparing end results with study goals. For instance, students can monitor themselves by asking their own questions or can accomplish this monitoring with others by trading questions. Students need to implement self-monitoring during learning, rather than at the last minute.

Svinicki's (2004) goal in creating the GAMES model was to guide learners to become more efficient. Each letter in the acronym refers to a component of good study behavior. Svinicki says that "students who follow this model are much more active in their learning and as a result process what they are learning at a deeper level" (p. 131). Her model was created for study habits in the face-to-face classroom. We adapted this model as a framework to develop the student survey for our study. Our intention in using this model was to discover the strategies that students used and how significant they were within the online environment.

In our study, participants were asked to select how often they used the 30 strategies based on the GAMES model, when they took online courses (on a scale on which the possible answers were "never," "rarely," "sometimes," "quite often," and "very often"). We interpreted the "never," "rarely," and "sometimes" responses as "no," and "quite often" and "very often" as "yes." A chi-square analysis was conducted to determine whether there was a statistical association between reported use of strategies and level of education (undergraduate versus graduate). Out of 30 strategies, 15 of them were statistically significant. The most popular strategies used by online students in our study were the following:

Active studying

- Mark electronically or highlight the text when reading. $(\chi^2 = 14.87; p < .001)$
- Pause periodically to summarize or paraphrase what was just studied. $(\chi^2 = 5.81; p < .016)$
- Look for connections between what is being studied at the moment and what was studied in the past. $(\chi^2 = 9.86; p < .002)$
- Write down questions to ask the instructor. $(\chi^2 = 10.55; p < .001)$
- Take breaks periodically to keep from getting too tired. $(\chi^2 = 5.31; p < .021)$

Meaning and memorable studying

- Make up own examples for concepts being learned. $(\chi^2 = 16.02; p < .001)$
- Put things into own words. $(\chi^2 = 4.71; p < .030)$
- Look for practical applications in real-life settings for the things being learned. $(\chi^2 = 20.15; p < .001)$

Explaining the materials in order to learn them

- Discuss the course content in the online group discussion forum. $(\chi^2 = 32.81; p < .001)$
- Answer questions in the online group discussion forum. $(\chi^2 = 47.48; p < .001)$
- Share course materials and receive feedback from online group. $(\chi^2 = 22.41; p < .001)$
- Collaborate with classmates in virtual teams. $(\chi^2 = 30.49; p < .001)$

Self-monitoring

- Make sure to answer own questions during studying. ($\chi^2 = 8.06; p < .005$)

- Work with another student to question each other's ideas. ($\chi^2 = 6.01; p < .014$)

- Have a range of strategies for learning; if one isn't working, try another one. ($\chi^2 = 4.84; p < .028$)

The selection of learning strategies generated noteworthy results. Although students did not select "goal-oriented study" strategies as important when identifying how often students used those strategies, in the open-ended questions, students actually described goal-oriented study strategies (setting goals and using strategies to achieve these goals) as very important for remaining motivated to learn.

When looking at undergraduate versus graduate students, we found that graduate students were more likely to use the 15 strategies just listed. A chi-square analysis was conducted to determine whether there was a statistical association between reported use of strategies and number of online courses taken. However, for students who had taken more than three online courses, only four strategies were statistically significant:

1. Taking breaks periodically to keep from getting too tired. ($\chi^2 = 7.27; p <. 007$)

2. Sharing course materials and receiving feedback from online group. ($\chi^2 = 5.59; p < .018$)

3. Collaborating with classmates in virtual teams. ($\chi^2 = 4.41; p < .036$)

4. Making sure to answer own questions during studying. ($\chi^2 = 4.56; p < .033$)

This result could mean that students who had taken more than three online courses had more experience, knew what to expect, and had already developed study strategies. Based on our findings, it appears as though students need to have a study plan to be successful.

We asked students to rate 12 strategies that most motivated them to participate in online courses in order of preference (with 1 being the strategy most preferred). We grouped these strategies into four categories: individual activities, group activities, mixed methods, and design preference. A chi-square analysis was conducted to determine whether there was a statistical association between reported preferences for strategies that most motivated students to participate in online courses and the level of education involved (undergraduate versus graduate). When looking at these four categories, undergraduate and graduate students showed statistically significantly different preferences in these strategies ($\chi^2 = 17.59; p < .001$).

These results show that undergraduate students were more likely to be motivated when completing individual or mixed activities. Graduate students were more likely to be motivated when completing group activities and when the course provided a specific design layout (for example, the course had a limited number of modules or units). The differences may be based on the course design (discipline, course format, interactive strategies, role of the instructor, technologies available, and support). Certain disciplines may be more content-focused and include more individual activities. Other disciplines may be more process-focused and include more group activities. The number of students in a given course may also influence the type of activities designed for the course. For example, courses that have 100 students are less likely to include group activities.

We also asked students to rate 16 learning strategies that kept them motivated to learn in an online course in order of preference (with 1 being the strategy most preferred). These learning strategies were grouped into four categories: (1) basic definition of concepts, (2) structural knowledge (how concepts go together), (3) application of concepts to problems, and (4) analysis of problem situations. A chi-square analysis was conducted to determine whether there was a statistical association between reported preferences for strategies that kept students most motivated to learn in online courses and the level of education involved (undergraduate versus graduate).

When one looks at these, four categories showed statistically significantly different preferences in these strategies ($\chi^2 = 11.15; p<.004$); undergraduate students were more likely to select strategies that provided basic definition of concepts (such as rehearsing, elaborating, organizing, and adding meaning), while graduate students were more likely to select strategies that provided structural knowledge (recognizing key ideas, organizing key ideas, and recognizing relationships among key ideas) and application of concepts (visualizing the process, developing process steps, rehearsing applying the process, and comparing versions of the process) (Svinicki, 2004). These differences may have occurred because graduate courses tend to be more focused on critical, creative, and complex thinking, rather than on basic thinking.

Students used time management, prioritizing, and learning strategies to achieve course goals. However, not all students have the skills to use these strategies. As instructors, we need to help students become aware of these strategies, realize their value, and put them into practice for a successful balance of their personal life, work, and school. We have observed that students who have control over their time and tasks are less likely to be controlled by the pace of their courses. In this way, students are setting the pace that works for them.

Prioritizing also gives students control through organizing and ranking tasks in order of importance. We have noticed that students who are successful in prioritizing tasks share their strategies and tools with others within the discussion area and follow a pattern of behavior throughout the course. For these students, we can predict when they will be online, how they will present the information (organization of documents), and how they will interact with others.

Having a study plan prior to the beginning of the online course can help students better achieve the learning goals, objectives, and outcomes of a course. The study plan will depend on how the instructor sets up the course and making the course available ahead of time. In this way, students have an opportunity to view the "big picture" of the course through the syllabus and create a study plan for the entire learning experience. We also build the learning modules into small chunks and release them as the course progresses. Students tell us they like this approach because they can see what is expected for the entire course, and at the same time they are not overwhelmed since the course content is distributed into discrete modules.

Rewards for Achieving Goals

The last element of the pathway that emerged from our study involves the rewards students obtain after achieving their course goal or goals. Students considered three types of rewards as motivators: academic, personal, and professional.

Academic Rewards Students in our study defined academic rewards as grades or extra credit. Students stated that they kept the idea in the back of their minds that they needed to get good grades. This idea helped them to stay motivated, or to "stay on top of everything," as one student said. If the subject matter was interesting, it made it even easier to stay motivated to get a good grade, according to the students. They knew that they needed "to complete the work on time in order to get a good grade," as several students stated, the same reason they did the work in their face-to-face courses. Extra credit was also another motivator that helped students persist because they knew that if they earned these extra credits earlier in the course, they might not have to work as hard at the end of the course and they would then have time to relax.

Students who do not see the relevance in the course assignments as a rewarding experience feel less likely to stay motivated in the course. For some students, lack of relevance can make assignments seem like busy work. As instructors, we learn about students' skill levels and interests during pre-course surveys and adjust course assignment options to meet students' needs. We also provide an explanation of the purpose of each assignment and its relevance to the course outcomes. One strategy we use to help students stay motivated in our online courses is to provide regular constructive feedback on assignments. Our feedback identifies strengths and weaknesses and helps students recognize their course progress and areas of improvement, while at the same time building self-esteem.

Personal Rewards   Students also considered personal rewards as motivators. One example of a personal reward was keeping in mind that personal activities or projects were things that could be done only when students had completed a certain amount of work. A few students called this a "reward system," something they wanted to do after they got their homework done, such as drink coffee, take a break, relax, or do something fun, as these students stated:

> . . . knowing that when I get it done, that I can do something else.

> [I] keep personal activities or projects as something that can only be done when a certain level of work has been met.

For some students in our online courses, having a checklist of course assignments helps them see when the small goals in the course are achieved and gives them a sense of personal satisfaction. We include, as part of each course module, the checklist feature within the learning management system so that students can keep track of their accomplishments. It is important to remind students that they need to take breaks, relax, and do something fun in between course tasks because this reminder can help them balance their academic and personal lives.

Professional Rewards The third type of reward was related to their professional work: getting a new job upon graduation and applying knowledge to their work or life. One student said this about what kept her motivated in the online course: "I always try to apply [knowledge] to my professional work. I see how it relates and how I can use the newfound knowledge." Another student explained, "I keep in mind the real-life problems that I am trying to solve and think about how what I am learning applies to them."

Applying what students learned and contemplating concepts as they related to their personal and professional experiences were essential for students in our study to feel that they had gotten something from their learning experiences. One student explained, "When I find something practical that I can utilize right away at my job, I [feel] more motivated to learn, to improve my skills, and [see the] potential in order to move up in my career."

One thing we do to encourage the sense of professional reward that a course assignment may provide is to share stories from students who have already taken the course and explain how they are using the skills taught in the course. One of our students said years later how much a specific online course had changed her perceptions about technology and her sense of confidence to support others. This example shows that rewards are not always immediate. By sharing stories, students can see the value of the course and its potential outcomes.

We also help students see the application of coursework to professional life through team projects, hands-on assignments, and internships. In some course assignments, we simulate the real-world experience so students can see the relevance of the skills learned. One online course that we taught involved the development, implementation, and evaluation of a Web conference. Students were part of a team to select conference focus and speakers, develop marketing strategies, plan conference logistics, implement the conference, and evaluate outcomes. This course was totally online through synchronous meetings and asynchronous discussions. Students were highly involved in all course tasks and motivated to accomplish the final course goal of implementing the Web conference. The evidence of their motivation was through hearing the excitement in their voices during synchronous meetings, their postings in the asynchronous discussions, the feedback to one another when course tasks were completed, and the quality of the materials they produced as a team.

EXPLAINING STUDY FINDINGS FROM A MOTIVATIONAL PERSPECTIVE

The findings of our study related to students' perspectives are reinforced by the literature on motivation. The pathway that emerged from our study shows the connection among students' beliefs, sense of control, and gains. When these three relate in an effective way, successful online learning may be predictable. It will depend on the individual's perceived self-efficacy, "beliefs in one's capabilities to organize and execute the courses of actions required to produce given attainments" (Bandura, 1997, p. 3).

Predictability promotes the ability to adapt to change. This requires a feeling of self-value and personal control. Perceived self-efficacy can involve control over one's motivation, thought processes, affective states, and actions; it can also mean the ability to change environmental conditions. For example, a new student decides to enter an online program but has no previous experience with online learning. This individual is unprepared for the new, elusive environment. Often this student's first reaction is to feel apprehensive, frustrated, and lost. To prevent this undesirable situation, the individual needs to be open and take control of cognitive, social, emotional, and behavioral skills. This student must believe in the power to produce results, otherwise there will be no attempt to make things happen. Belief is the key factor.

Students are more likely to be motivated and successful in online learning if they have control over their perceptions of skills and strategies. Motivation is what can inspire them to initiate, guide, and maintain their goal-oriented behaviors. According to Bandura (1986), motivation can be either biologically based or cognitively based. Biologically based motivation relates to what the body reacts to. For example, in the face-to-face environment, we as instructors can more easily motivate students by using our senses and appealing to their senses, since we are all in the same room. However, in the online environment, we need to adapt our senses. To motivate students, part of the solution can be designing instruction that takes the senses into consideration and uses strategies to provide students with a sense of satisfaction through external incentives.

Cognitively based motivation relates to the image we create in our minds of what we expect can be changed into motivators of our behavior. In this case, the initiator to action is anticipated instead of the actual incentive. The expected results may be in the form of something that is material, sensory, symbolic, or social. Another way to look at cognitively based motivation is through the influences of internal values and one's responses to one's own performance. Here, goals and values serve as cognitive representations of desired outcomes. Self-incentives play a role in giving direction to action and help the individual persist in the effort to meet the goal (Bandura, 1996). For example, an individual enrolls in an online program to get a promotion at work. The initiator to action is the desire to achieve a goal. The incentive is increased salary through the promotion.

Bandura (1986) says that incentives can be intrinsic or extrinsic. Intrinsic incentives come from within (such as self-feedback) and are the ones that are most rewarding and long-lasting. Intrinsic incentives are based on self-value. Extrinsic incentives come from without, involve rewards, and decline in interest when the rewards are no longer present. We know that intrinsic motivation can be cultivated and that self-perception can be changed through learning. In the example of the new student who had just entered the online program, the apprehensiveness, frustration, and feeling of loss could be changed through task-contingent incentives and competency-contingent incentives.

When students are given directions to complete a course task of high interest and receive a good grade, they are motivated to persist in the course. When students in a team have to complete a developmental project, they work through the tasks involved one by one. As students progress through the project, they gain new competencies through extrinsic incentives. Students must be provided with tools of self-directedness to promote development and stability that progressively build on their skills.

When we teach online courses, we provide constructive feedback on team tasks that build on the skills students are acquiring. Our feedback focuses on team strengths and areas for enhancement. When students lack the appropriate skills for the task, they are allowed to revise what they have done. In this way, students can gradually become more proficient by focusing on their progress.

Incentives are different from rewards. Incentives motivate someone to persist in completing an online course. Rewards are the recognition of effort or achievement upon completion of the course. For an online course, the incentive would be task completion for each unit. The reward would be getting a good grade for completing the task. In this case, the capability to self-motivate and purposefully act is rooted in cognitive activity (Bandura, 1997) in the online environment. When students can help shape the incentives within a course, it has value for them. Conversely, when incentives are imposed and students have no part in shaping the course, they are more likely to resist. In addition, when students have long-term goals, they need to create sub-goals and self-evaluation incentives in order to continually motivate themselves (Bandura, 1986).

Another concept in the motivation literature that is often mentioned is having a positive attitude toward reaching a goal. Even though participants in our study did not directly mention having a positive attitude toward the online course, the positive attitude was embedded in the learning process. Otherwise these students would not have stayed in the course. Wlodkowski (2008) says that developing a positive attitude requires both relevance and volition. An online course that has irrelevant assignments can be a frustrating experience for students. In this case, students are more likely to make a conscious decision (volition) to drop out of a course.

One concern about today's generation is that too much emphasis is placed on the grade or the final outcome of an assignment, and praise of the process along the way is neglected. For example, instructors often say, "Great that you have achieved an 'A'!" Such praise is for the outcome, rather than the process. A better way to provide incentives, particularly in our fast-changing world, is through praise during the process as students work to complete a task. For example, instructors might say, "I really like the way you solved the problem in the case study!" In this praise, students hear how they are doing along the way, building their self-esteem and helping them to feel more confident to go on to the next problem. This perspective gives students a different way of thinking, feeling, and acting. Dweck (2007) calls this a "growth mindset," which is "based on the belief that [the] basic qualities are things [that] can [be cultivated] through efforts. Although people may differ in every which way—in their initial talents and aptitudes, interests, or temperaments—everyone can change and grow through application and experience" (p. 12). As students believe that they can change and grow, they become more self-assured of their learning process.

It is important for us as instructors to understand what influences students' capabilities for staying in online courses. One of the main influences is having a positive attitude. Another is individuals' perceived self-value, which gives them control over their motivation, thought processes, affective states, and actions. By knowing what is happening in the students' minds, instructors can envision how students will behave. Instructors can then design an online environment that promotes adjustment to change. By designing an online environment that gives students control over their perceptions of skills and strategies, instructors can inspire and motivate them.

Intrinsic and extrinsic incentives also influence students' capabilities for staying in online courses. Because intrinsic incentives can have an impact on motivation, strategies that encourage students' self-value can be incorporated into the course design. To further motivate students, instructors can include rewards within the course design as extrinsic incentives.

INCORPORATING STUDENT STRATEGIES INTO COURSE DESIGN

We know that students drop out of online courses because of feeling isolated, having technology failure, and experiencing lack of instructor feedback or support (Abel, 2005; Motteram & Forrester, 2005; Palloff & Pratt, 1999). We also know that the lack of skill level, motivation, and support can be barriers to student learning and affect their persistence in online courses (Muilenburg & Berge, 2005). However, certain factors help determine what is needed to retain students and reduce dropout. Students' perceptions about their online participation are important indicators of how well they will do in a course. Looking at students' characteristics and skills, prior to admission to an online program or enrolling in an online course, can help instructors implement appropriate strategies and support students' online learning experiences (Rovai, 2003).

Two other indicators that can help instructors determine intervention methods for a successful online learning experience are external and internal factors after starting an online course. External factors are those in which students may have personal and professional roles that conflict with academic roles, such as being a parent or a full-time worker. Internal factors are those students need to overcome, such as a lack of self-esteem, social integration, and ready access to instructor support (Rovai, 2003). By being aware of these factors, instructors can delineate strategies to help students persist in their online courses.

Strategies for successful online learning are those that are learner-centered, respond to students' needs, provide consistency and relevance, and create interactive and engaging environments. Table 3.1 provides a list of strategies that students in our study identified to keep them motivated and persist in online courses. The table also includes ways to incorporate these strategies into the course design.

Table 3.1. Ways to Incorporate Motivating Strategies into Course Design

Student Strategies for Staying Motivated	Ways to Incorporate Motivating Strategies into Course Design
Self-awareness Awareness of learning process, situation, and consequences of not moving forward	Use icebreakers to self-reflect on their interests and background and how they relate to the course
	Share stories from previous students about how they are applying learning from this course
	Conduct student surveys to assess learning styles, technology skills, and content knowledge level
	Emphasize course rubrics and grading to demonstrate course expectations and consequences
Self-efficacy Belief that one is capable of organizing, putting into action, and moving ahead to complete a course	Use a scavenger hunt for students to navigate the online course during orientation activities
	Guide students to review course assignments in syllabus
	Ask students to create a study plan for the course
	Monitor students' participation through learning analytics during first weeks of course to verify if students are progressing effectively and efficiently
Goal for taking a course	Ask students to identify goal(s) for taking the course during orientation activities
Setting small goals during the course	Create a checklist of specific tasks students need to accomplish during each module
Means to achieve goals *Time management* Efficient methods and skills to achieve goals and accomplish course tasks	Distribute a handout to students with strategies to more efficiently achieve course goals and accomplish tasks. Include in the handout the following strategies:
	• Conduct online work every day at a scheduled time.
	• Have a structured schedule.
	• Stay on schedule with readings and postings.
	• Set aside time as if in a face-to-face class.

- Block out specific time per class for doing readings, contributions to discussion, and homework.
- Allow days off from doing online work.
- Stay a week ahead in assignments.
- Check on the course frequently.
- Designate quiet time to better concentrate on the online course.
- Create a timeline with details, due dates, and deadlines for the online course.
- Plan ahead, set deadlines and time based on role as full-time worker, parent, or full-time student.

Remind students that they are in control over their academic and personal lives. These strategies are effective by helping students have control over their time, rather than time controlling them. Check Exhibit 3.1 for a sample handout.

Means to achieve goals
Prioritizing Identifying tasks and ranking them in order of importance

Distribute a handout to students with strategies to better identify tasks and rank order them. Include in the handout the following strategies:

- Use a planner or a calendar to purposefully schedule time or tasks for the course based on due dates.
- Organize documents, save them with specific names, print off reading materials and keep them in a binder or digital folder.
- Highlight when major tasks are due, set a goal start date, and look at gaps in the schedule.
- Have a plan prior to the start of each week.
- Develop an organization chart to envision the course step-by-step.

Check Exhibit 3.2 for a sample handout.

Continued

Table 3.1. Continued

Student Strategies for Staying Motivated	Ways to Incorporate Motivating Strategies into Course Design
Means to achieve goals *Learning strategies* Methods for learning content and procedures that influence student's study habits.	Distribute a handout to students with strategies to learn content and procedures. Include in the handout the following strategies: • Mark electronically or highlight the text when reading. • Pause periodically to summarize or paraphrase what has been studied. • Look for connections between present and past content. • Write down questions for the instructor. • Take breaks periodically to keep from getting too tired. • Make up own examples for concepts while learning. • Use own words. • Look for practical applications in real-life settings for things being learned. • Discuss the course content and answer others' questions in the online group discussion forums. • Share course materials and receive feedback from the online group. • Collaborate with classmates in virtual teams. • Answer own questions while studying. • Question someone else's ideas. Check Exhibit 3.3 for a sample handout.
Rewards for achieving goals Rewards can assist students in achieving a goal or goals within a course (academic), give them pleasure after completing course tasks (personal), or help them put into practice what they have learned (professional).	Provide regular constructive individual feedback on assignments to help students identify academic progress Allow for extra credit early in the course as a motivator for accomplishing tasks and reducing anxiety later Recognize strengths and weaknesses when giving individual feedback on assignments so that students can feel good about their progress, improve, and build self-esteem Remind students that they need to take breaks, relax, and do something fun in between tasks or work. This can help them balance academic and personal life Help students see the application of coursework to professional life through team projects, hands-on assignments, and internships

---

Exhibit 3.1.
Time Management Strategies

- Conduct online work every day at a scheduled time.
- Have a structured schedule.
- Stay on schedule with readings and postings.
- Set aside time as if in a face-to-face class.
- Block out specific time per class for doing readings, contributions to discussion, and homework.
- Allow days off from doing online work.
- Stay a week ahead in assignments.
- Check on the course frequently.
- Designate quiet time to better concentrate on the online course.
- Create a timeline with details, due dates, and deadlines for the online course.
- Plan ahead, set deadlines and time based on roles as full-time worker, parent, or full-time student.

Exhibit 3.2.
Prioritizing Strategies

- Use a planner or a calendar to purposefully schedule time or tasks for the course based on due dates.
- Organize documents, save them with specific names, print off reading materials, and keep them in a binder or digital folder.
- Highlight when major tasks are due, set a goal start date, and look at gaps in the schedule.
- Have a plan prior to the start of each week.
- Develop an organization chart to envision the course step by step.

The next chapter addresses three types of support strategies that students in our study perceived as important for staying motivated in online courses. Then, Chapter 4 presents strategies related to these types of support that instructors can incorporate into the course design to retain students in their online courses. Chapter 4 also provides examples of support services from institutions of higher education.

Exhibit 3.3.
Learning Strategies

- Mark electronically or highlight the text when reading.
- Pause periodically to summarize or paraphrase what has been studied.
- Look for connections between present and past content.
- Write down questions for the instructor.
- Take breaks periodically to keep from getting too tired.
- Make up own examples for concepts while learning.
- Use own words.
- Look for practical applications in real-life settings for things being learned.
- Discuss the course content and answer others' questions in the online group discussion forums.
- Share course materials and receive feedback from the online group.
- Collaborate with classmates in virtual teams.
- Answer own questions while studying.
- Question someone else's ideas.

Support Strategies for Helping Online Students Persist

Studies about online education have indicated that support is essential for retaining students in online courses. Findings show that support can be provided through instructor assistance (Chyung & Vachon, 2005) or the institution (Muilenburg & Berge, 2005). In our study, students also considered having self-care as important for keeping them motivated to persist in online courses.

Successful online learning depends on strategic course design, interactive and engaging teaching strategies, and sound support. Support means creating an environment that is conducive to learning, developing strategies that create community engagement, and incorporating assistance throughout the process. Support provides students a sense of community, which allows them to avoid the feeling of isolation; gives students a sense of self-direction and management, thus reducing loss of control; contributes to learner satisfaction; and increases motivation, helping students persist in an online course.

When the instructor is aware of the necessary support strategies for online students, there is a better chance that students will feel confident and persist until the end of the course. This chapter addresses three types of support that students in our study perceived as important for staying motivated in online courses. Then the chapter presents strategies related to these types of support that instructors can use to retain students in their online courses.

TYPES OF SUPPORT PERCEIVED AS IMPORTANT BY STUDENTS

Students in our study perceived receiving support and taking care of themselves as important for staying motivated in online courses. Students identified three types of support to help them stay engaged in the online course, complete coursework, and maintain a balance in their lives: human resource support, institutional support, and self-care.

Human Resource Support

Human resource support was provided by instructors, other students, family, and friends through various forms of communication. Support from instructors was offered via e-mail, Skype, the discussion board and grading area in the learning management system, and social media (Twitter, blogs, and so on). Instructor support was given to clarify course issues, answer questions related to course materials, informally communicate with students about personal matters that might have affected course progress, and assess student work through feedback. Instructor presence either informally or formally was an essential aspect of student retention. Also, students perceived quick response from instructors as critical to staying motivated in the online course, so that students knew how they were progressing. According to two of the participants in our study, instructor support helped guide their learning or predict what to do next:

> I look forward to reading feedback after I post a discussion from the instructor. This either solidifies or guides understanding of the course concepts.

> I am not afraid to ask the instructor questions. I like to stay ahead of [the] game . . . be one of the first to post so all the ideas are not taken.

For one student, instructor support was not so different from face-to-face support: "[Support was] much the same as a traditional course, I will send the instructor a private message or e-mail for clarification, unless it relates to a discussion topic." When instructors did not respond, lacked presence in the course, or used language that was too formal, students reacted with negative comments such as these:

> I don't really have any [support strategies]; I have tried communicating extra with my professors but they rarely respond in a helpful way.

> I rarely find educators who are willing to "speak" in mainstream terms and prefer to use complicated vocabulary and dialog which is NOT helpful to me. OR worse, educators who repeat what they have already written. This does NOT help me at all.

Support from other students was very much appreciated. Learning from other students not only offered a sense of community, but also provided quick answers and solutions to course issues. A number of students said that the discussion forums and e-mail were the most important support methods for them in their online courses. For example, this student said, "I use the discussion boards when I'm having trouble [and] a fellow student will reply with help." Many of the participants stated that they relied on their teammates a lot and learned from them too, as this student implied: "I tend to learn more from [other students] than from the course materials alone." Based on our study findings, a sense of community learning and peer support was vital to keeping students engaged in the online course.

One example from our own experience in which peer support helped motivate student learning was a course that involved a book review on current technologies. Students were distributed into groups based on the book they selected to complete the review. One book focused on virtual environments. A suggestion was made by the instructor for students to experience the type of technology contained in the book that they were reading. One student in one group had experience working with Second Life, a technology that provides an online virtual environment. This student took leadership in inviting group members to experience how the technology worked. Although the instructor had made the suggestion, it was this student who encouraged others to learn about the technology. This type of peer support gave a different dimension to the activity in this course.

Students reflected in the discussion area of the course about how motivated they were for the activity and the sense of presence they felt. One student said that she was motivated to try Second Life for the purpose of exploring its potential. There was a feeling of excitement to "meet" her group members in the virtual environment, too. She also felt a sense of "being there" and "being with" others during the virtual field trip. Another student also wanted to "meet" her team members in the virtual environment. This student felt a sense of presence by hearing others' voices and interacting with them. In the reflection, the student said that she thought they had a good team and was glad she was able to experience Second Life with the team. Students appreciated the support of the student who walked them through the virtual environment. It was evident through the student reflections in the discussion area that the activity was worthwhile and enriched the learning experience of the group.

Another type of support that students considered important to stay motivated in an online course was from others outside the online class, like family and friends. Family and friends supported students who participated in our study in completing home tasks, encouraged students in their courses, shared tips and techniques from other online courses, and reminded students of the work they needed to do. The following quotes reflect this type of support for our study participants:

> [I received] encouragement from my family—they are instrumental support with my son, and emotional support when I'm feeling overwhelmed.

> While taking online courses, my family picks up slack with regards to cleaning or laundry.

> [I have] someone else who can take care of household chores [while I am doing coursework].

> I find support in my fellow students as well as my husband who is also a graduate student. It is good to have a support community of people who are going through and experiencing what you are.

> [I] hook up with someone else that I can talk to outside of the online experience, or that I knew from another course.

> [I have] friends remind me of my work.

In addition to instructor and classroom peer support, students expressed a need to have support from family and friends. This support, outside of students' online experience, helped students feel less overwhelmed and more a part of a larger community, removing a sense of loneliness.

Institutional Support

Institutional support included services provided by the institution to assist the students to access information, seek technical help, and solve learning deficiencies. Students in our study considered institutional support to be important because it helped them easily access campus resources and services to complete their coursework. Many of these support services were embedded into the learning management system as links or available in the institutional website. Students stated that they could also reach these services via telephone or in person. Students used the library resources to conduct searches, to access electronic reserve documents, and to download or borrow books or articles. In some cases, a dedicated librarian and a Web page for online students to use in their research were available.

One of the institutional support services students in our study identified was technology support through a help desk. Students used the help desk to inquire about and resolve technical problems. In this instance, a message board was available for questions and answers. Quick responses from support services were appreciated by students in our study and decreased their frustrations. Another type of support that was mentioned was related to student services such as special needs, writing center, mentoring, and so on. Having available resources and consultation beyond just the instructor was an effective strategy for students in our study.

In our experience, often we have to remind students that they can seek help from other resources on campus instead of becoming frustrated with the technology. For example, students new to the online environment are not able to search library databases efficiently and feel at a loss. We refer them to the chat area within the library for immediate support. Another situation that happens is when students lack skills in using basic word processing software. We refer them to the frequently asked questions (FAQs) section, the online tutorials within the institution, or the help desk to speak with a staff member. To reinforce these areas of support, we incorporate direct links within the learning management system, so that students are one click away from support.

Accessibility is another area in which students may need support and which instructors frequently overlook. In our courses, we have had to adapt materials to meet the special needs of our students. Blind students use special readers to follow course materials. We describe all the visuals in the course, and when videos and graphics are posted on the Web, we describe them in text, so that the screen reader can electronically read what is displayed. For deaf students, we always include closed captioning for video and audio presentations.

We are also careful when we conduct synchronous meetings using the video, audio, and chat features in a Web conferencing system to explain course information or do a presentation. For example, when the course includes a foreign language speaker, we encourage students to let us know if the accent of the speaker is limiting their participation. We ask participants to speak more slowly or post the information in the chat area. We also repeat through voice what is being written in the chat area as a strategy to meet the needs of sight-impaired students and as a way to create interactivity and presence. This approach is not only for students with special needs, but also for all students in the course.

Self-Care

In our study, students defined self-care as the ability to reflect on and be self-aware of their own strengths and weaknesses, and to act upon them. Self-care meant taking care of their own health and having good study habits. Self-care required them to be self-aware and to reflect on what was necessary to help them stay motivated and persist in the online course. Eating well, sleeping, and exercising were practices incorporated into students' daily lives to bring balance and success. One participant called these practices "me time." Another participant said, "The best support strategy was getting enough sleep. I go to bed early and wake up refreshed and ready to learn." "Isolation both from other people as well as from digital distractions" was also a way they could take time for themselves away from class.

Although the participants in our study shared only a few stories about self-care, we have heard many stories from our own students. We have noticed that once students in our online courses trust one another in the course conversations, they tend to share personal strategies they use for work-life balance. Students say that, regardless of the work involved in an online course, they need to set limits on how much time they spend online during the course to avoid burnout. One student we had in an online course did burn out. She failed to balance her work and personal life. Throughout the course, she did not meet deadlines for synchronous meetings, asynchronous discussions, and project deadlines. She was always behind on assignments, which further affected her performance in the course. This student had already taught online and thought she could easily go through the course based on her previous online experience. She later shared that the low grade in the course made her reassess her work-life balance. She explained that she was overextending herself by working full time, taking other online courses, being highly involved in community work, and dedicating time to her family. Her unrealistic expectations of work, school, and personal time and tasks caused burnout. As a result, she temporarily quit her job, pulled back from her community involvement, and focused primarily on her family and herself before making a decision to return to her job.

In contrast to this story is the experience of a freshman student who took online courses and initially felt overwhelmed. With assistance from family members, she was able to look at the whole picture of being a new college student and create a plan to ensure that she was taking care of herself as well as completing her work. She developed a comprehensive chart that included all of her coursework, study time, part-time job, family affairs, and self-care activities such as exercise, meals, sleeping, and meditation time. This chart was initially developed as a visual image of her life at that point in time. The chart helped her create study habits, differentiate between work and personal life, and set aside time to take care of herself. After a while this routine became intuitive, and it was not necessary for her to continue to use the chart on a regular basis.

Balancing school, work, and personal life is an essential skill for anyone. The two examples we shared when taking online courses show how self-care through reflection can help students understand their strengths and weaknesses and find ways to act upon them. As instructors, we need to remind students that self-care is also part of being an online learner. What we can do to assist students is to refer them to campus and online resources that can help them balance their mental, physical, and regular habits.

SUPPORT STRATEGIES FOR HELPING ONLINE STUDENTS PERSIST

Based on students' perceptions of receiving support and instructors' experience and practice in our study, plus our own experience, we suggest three support strategies for retaining students in online courses: instructional, institutional, and self-care.

Instructional Support Strategies

When we create online courses, the course design sets the framework for the interactions to occur. When we teach the course, we implement and incorporate instructional support strategies by doing the following:

- Creating activities that orient students to the course and help them meet each other and develop trust and community
- Providing a syllabus that shows the "big picture" of the course
- Embedding links to other resources within the learning management system
- Including forums for formal and informal conversations
- Providing individual and group feedback
- Being flexible to accommodate students' needs

One of our colleagues shared an example of providing instructional support to one of her students. This example involved a student who entered the online program with a negative attitude because she learned that she had to take more courses than she had previously understood. She also had poor technology skills. She was, however, motivated to take the online courses to become recertified in her field. During the online learning experience, the student struggled to use the technology, meet course requirements, and find time to work on the online course and respond regularly to the instructor. Throughout this experience, the instructor worked closely with the student by contacting the student when she did not respond, providing instructions on how to use the technology, giving an extension for the assignments, and allowing the student to retake the exam. Because of the student's extrinsic motivation and instructor support, the student was able to successfully complete the course and receive her recertification.

This student did not realize during the course how much support was provided to her until she reflected on her online learning experience after she had completed the courses to receive her recertification. It appears that this student was overwhelmed for several reasons. The first reason was that she had to take more courses than she had expected. Second, she was new to online learning and the use of technology. Third, she was heavily involved with work tasks during the period of the course. Because of these circumstances, the student noticed how much support was provided to her only when she reflected on her online learning experience. The evidence of her reflection was in the form of a thank-you letter to the instructor expressing gratitude and appreciation for her support. In this example, the instructor incorporated instructional support strategies by being flexible in meeting the student's needs.

This example shows how important it is for the instructor to have clear communication with students, be present and available to students, and respond quickly to their inquiries. Like our colleague, we also provide instructional support through administrative, facilitative, and evaluative tasks (Conceição & Lehman, 2011).

The entry to an online course can be a "make it or break it" experience for the student. Before the course begins, we send out a welcome letter to set the tone of instructional support for students. Our students say that the welcome letter makes them feel that the instructor really wants to get to know them as an individual. We also use icebreakers during orientation to the course before the course starts or during the first week of the course as a support strategy. These icebreakers help students meet each other and build trust and community. The icebreakers take different forms, including creating a map where we ask students "where in the world they are located," a group album with pictures and biographies using PowerPoint, or a vanity license plate where students provide metaphors for their online experiences. During this time, students are introduced to the "big picture" of the course through the syllabus and learn how to navigate the online environment and create a mental image of the course expectations. To help students have easy access to outside resources, we embed links to other resources within the learning management system.

During the course, our instructional support related to administrative tasks takes the form of communication and clarification of course assignments through announcements, management and monitoring of student progress through the technology, basic technical support, and psychological and emotional assistance. In content-related forums, our instructional support tasks are facilitative and involve encouraging students to participate in the content discussion, providing insights on students' contributions, and sharing resources and soliciting comments. The evaluative tasks consist of giving individual feedback on assignments or group feedback on projects. As we accomplish these tasks, we keep in mind that we must be flexible to accommodate students' needs. Table 4.1 details specific instructional support strategies to incorporate into the online course in the form of tasks.

Table 4.1. Instructional Support Strategies for Online Courses

Instructional Support Strategies	How to Incorporate Strategies When Teaching the Course
Welcome letter	Send letter 1–2 weeks before course begins
Icebreakers	Have students participate in icebreaker activities during class orientation
Communication and clarification of course assignments	Send out announcements as needed in the form of audio, video, or text
Management and monitoring of student progress	Review course learning analytics to check student progress. Send personal messages to students regarding their access, technology usage, and performance in the course as needed
Technical support	Send out announcements to solve technology issues, respond to technology questions in help forums, or remind students to seek help from campus resources
Psychological and emotional assistance	Send individual e-mails to students when they lack confidence, show low self-esteem, or are unable to express feelings during online discussions
Insights on contributions	Give constructive feedback on content contributions through acknowledgement, praise, and encouragement
Sharing of resources and solicitation of comments	Expand students' content learning by inviting guest speakers with up-to-date information, current news, or relevant events. In the discussion area, challenge students through questions and request responses
Individual feedback on assignments	Provide individual feedback upon completion of an assignment within 7–10 days, so that students can see their progress in the course. Feedback comments can be posted in the grades area of the learning management system or sent via e-mail
Group feedback on projects	Provide group feedback on project tasks as the course progresses via e-mail or within the group discussion area

Institutional Support Strategies

It is important to incorporate institutional support into the course design. Institutional support involves using available campus resources to help students succeed in an online course. To accomplish this aim, we need to communicate to students available support services within our institutions.

Support services in higher education are part of a system. This system includes the process that starts prior to admission to a program or course and lasts until after graduation. In this process, students feel that they belong to a program and are being socially integrated. The support services that an institution of higher education can offer may fall into one of three categories: institutional, instructional, and student.

Institutional Services   Institutional services involve student admission, course scheduling, financial aid, registration process, and student personnel records and accounts. These services are the first contact the students have with the institution. Often instructors are not aware of how these services function. It is important for instructors at least to know contact information for these services, so that instructors can inform prospective and current students where to go for help.

Instructional Services   Instructional services are the ones that address standards for academics, advising, testing, remedial support, special needs, library, bookstore, and technical support. This type of support is used by students after admission to a program and is instrumental in retaining students. These services provide support for determining the program of study, course schedule, assessment of previous knowledge, and placement at the appropriate level of competency. Other services, such as mentoring and tutoring, assist students in areas in which they are deficient and need remedial support. For students with disabilities, the special needs office is available to mediate those demands. Exhibit 4.1 provides an example of the use of synchronous communication to support online students in higher education. Online tutoring is described as an important strategy to actively engage students in remedial support and course clarification and comprehension.

The PASS technology described in Exhibit 4.1 provides benefits for students in a variety of ways. First, it gives an easy access link for students within the learning management system (D2L). Easy access allows students to avoid searching

Exhibit 4.1.
Use of Synchronous Communication to Support Online Students

One example of online tutoring services is the University of Wisconsin-Milwaukee's Panther Academic Support Services (PASS). PASS offers in-person tutoring and supplemental instruction for first- and second-year gateway courses using synchronous Web conferencing—two-way video, two-way audio, and chat features for fast, easy online interactions.

One hundred peer tutors and supplemental instruction leaders (juniors, seniors, and graduate students in their field of study) provide support services to online students. These tutors have a strong background in the field, have taken the courses they provide tutoring for, and are trained in the features of *Blackboard Collaborate*, which offer blended technologies and interactive sessions that include polling, file transfer, whiteboard tools, and Web-touring features.

PASS manages five course sites in *Desire2Learn* (D2L) for tutoring in mathematics, science, social science, humanities, and business. *Blackboard Collaborate* is embedded into D2L. Students enrolled in first- and second-year courses in these subjects are added to these tutoring sites. "Online Rooms" is a tab on the navigation bar, which allows access to synchronous communication through *Blackboard Collaborate*. Access to these services is only provided to those students enrolled at the University. These students are notified of times and directions on how to access their sessions through e-mails sent out from the D2L site.

Tutors have the flexibility to conduct weekly individual or group online sessions, online exam reviews, or both. Two-hour online exam reviews draw over 100 students in blended and online formats. To meet the increasing use of tutoring services, PASS has student technology assistants who monitor chat board questions for the tutor, answer technology questions, and help ensure a smoothly running session.

Tutoring sessions are recorded and archived by *Blackboard Collaborate* for further review by the students. The archives are widely used beyond the actual participants since they are made public. Tutors also review their own sessions at the end of each semester to identify short clips of key concepts or study tips from their courses. These clips are captured by special software (*Jing* or *Camtasia*) by the PASS technology team and placed in the content section of the PASS D2L site for future reviewing.

Johanna Dvorak, Ph.D., Director, Educational Support Services, University of Wisconsin-Milwaukee (UWM) (http://pass.uwm.edu)

separately for information and resources and is a time saver. Second, the instructional service utilizes similar communication technologies that students use on a regular basis in their personal lives or workplace (such as instant messaging and e-mail). Third, by offering online tutoring with human contact, students can feel a sense of closeness and personalization. With these services, this institution is making its support as transparent as it is in the traditional environment.

Students at a distance need access to the same content resources as face-to-face students, such as online tutoring, the library, and the bookstore. Having a dedicated tutor and library staff to provide this support can eliminate some of the anxiety that comes with learning online. The bookstore is also an important resource for students to access content materials and should have books available ahead of time and available for online purchase. Technology support is critical for the online learner, because without technology there is no class. Having easy access to a help desk can reduce tension and frustration throughout the course. Instructors play an important role in coordinating and communicating what is available to students.

Student Services Student services include personal assistance to students throughout their program or courses. These services begin with an orientation to general online learning, which is often self-paced and available on the online program's website. This orientation provides opportunities for students to identify their online readiness, become familiar with the asynchronous and synchronous technologies they will be using, and learn about the institution and the different services available. These institutional services vary from career advice, health and wellness, and personal counseling, to ethical and legal services. Exhibit 4.2 provides a student service example. This example focuses on intentionally designing an orientation course in the beginning of an online program.

As set out in Exhibit 4.2, EriksonOnline provides a well-orchestrated orientation prior to the beginning of an online program. This orientation benefits students by helping them gain confidence, making the technology transparent, and building community as students become members of the program. Thus, as students begin the new program, the focus is on learning rather than on the technology.

One area of concern for us as online programs expand to include international students is how to serve these students and better meet their support needs, since they reside in other countries. As one of us is involved in international student

Learning How to Learn Online: Supporting Early and Persistent Success for New Online Students

An example of an effective student service is the one at Erickson Institute. Erikson Institute has developed EriksonOnline, a customized online teaching and learning environment built on the *Blackboard Learn* platform and developed specifically for the master's degree in early childhood education. The Institute has a deep understanding of the needs of adult learners who are new to online learning and have limited technology experience. This has led to a highly effective, engaging, and empowering online approach within a consistent and user-friendly environment.

Students entering this graduate program are required to be teaching full time in the classroom and to have at least three years of classroom teaching experience. These teachers bring a wealth of knowledge and experience to the online learning community, but begin the process with little or no skills in online learning.

As part of an extensive orientation to the program, the Distance Learning Team (comprised of instructional designers and a media specialist) developed the Learning with EriksonOnline course. Built in the same EriksonOnline environment used in the courses, the orientation includes a video-based guided tour of the environment and a "treasure hunt" activity. This activity includes a checklist for new online learners to visit the essential areas of the course environment. As learners navigate through the orientation, they try out the tools they will need for participating and contributing to the learning community when the courses begin.

Two weeks before the start of the semester, new online learners are also given access to the Learning with EriksonOnline course and the course information areas of their enrolled courses. The information includes: a welcome and course introduction video from the instructor, syllabus, readings, assignments, participation guidelines, and grading policies. During this time, students are encouraged to work through a series of technology checks, guided experiences, and video tutorials that help them navigate through the online environment. Students are also able to practice using the essential tools needed on the first day of class, including course mail, discussion posts, blogs, opening and viewing video clips, listening to narrated PowerPoint presentations, opening PDFs, downloading resources, and asking questions in the *Ask the Distance Learning Team* open discussion.

Community building begins during the orientation when students are encouraged to share a photo and post a bio for the cohort photo album. They also view photos, video introductions, and bios of the online faculty and Erikson staff involved in designing, developing, and delivering the online courses. The expectation of participation and contributions to the online learning community are built into the orientation process from the moment new online students receive their username, password, and login information.

Another essential feature of EriksonOnline is that help is never more than a click away, and online learners also have one click access to the Academic Success Center and to the Student Services from the EriksonOnline page. As part of the orientation process students are guided to these resources and complete specific tasks that ensure that they are familiar with the resources and assistance available to them.

A few days before classes begin, the Distance Learning Team hosts a Learning with EriksonOnline synchronous webinar that includes a chance for new students to meet the instructional designers and tech support specialists they will work with throughout their academic program. They are provided with a real-time guided tour through the environment and demonstrations of the online learning tools with opportunities to ask questions and solve technical issues before class begins in a low stakes synchronous experience. And it is a chance to login to the webinar platform and practice with managing audio and Web cams.

Embedded in the orientation activities and resources in the Learning with EriksonOnline course are tips and resources for successful online learning. Time management, study skills, how to participate in an online discussion, and how to contribute to the online learning community, are examples of the kinds of learning support strategies that help online students gain confidence in a new and unfamiliar learning environment.

Chip Donohue, Erikson Institute, Chicago (http://www.erikson.edu)

recruitment, it became apparent that institutional, instructional, and student services support should be considered when admitting international students. As online contact with international students increases, we ask the following questions when identifying institutional, instructional, and student services:

Institutional services

- *Admission process:* How long does it take for the admission process? Will it require a longer time to submit translated student information?
- *Tuition payment:* How can foreign students carry out tuition payments?
- *Program validation:* How is the program validated in different countries?

Instructional services

- *Bookstore:* How long will it take the books to reach the foreign destination? What type of payment can students use to purchase books?
- *Remedial:* What kind of support will international students need for writing, tutoring, and mentoring?
- *Testing:* Is there a requirement in other countries for proctored exams? What arrangements are necessary in foreign countries for proctoring exams?

Student services

- *Time zones:* How can services to students be accommodated to different time zones?

- *Program orientation:* Does the program orientation provide guidelines for students in other countries?

- *Counseling services:* Can students in other countries use the counseling services within the institution? Is the staff prepared for assisting the international students?

Institutional support through institutional, instructional, and student services is generally available but not always visible for online students. It is the responsibility of the instructor to make students aware of institutional support services and incorporate them into their online courses. To do so requires pre-planning, coordination, and clear communication. When incorporated into a course, these services can be aggregated into categories and linked by means of a tab within the learning management system. In some cases, the instructional design team of an institution or college include these services as part of the course template in the learning management system.

Self-Care Strategies

One theme that emerged from the students who participated in our study was self-care, which involved taking care of themselves or requesting assistance from others. This type of support was not part of the scheduled course activities and time and involved self-reflection, self-management, self-discipline, and self-direction.

In our experience, we have noted that students who have taken several online courses have a better understanding of the whole picture of learning online. They see the value of integrating mental, physical, and regular habits of self-care throughout their course period in order to balance their life and work and maintain quality of life. Mental habits can be practiced from anywhere and at no cost. They can help students by doing the following:

- Providing students with attentive awareness of the reality of the present moment and helping students clarify their minds

- Assisting students with clear comprehension of whatever is taking place and providing students a way to be calmly aware of themselves, their feelings, thoughts, perceptions, and consciousness
- Supporting students in self-analysis, which can result in increased wisdom and enhance discernment
- Helping students reduce stress, bring inner peace and emotional well-being, and gain new perspectives

Physical habits involve consistent exercising such as doing yoga or Pilates, walking, running, swimming, and weight training. Consistent exercise can help students control their weight, combat disease and other conditions, improve mood and emotions, boost energy, promote better sleeping, have fun, and improve their learning.

Regular habits such as sleeping well, periodic breaks, healthy eating, social time, laughter and humor, watching TV, and listening to music can help students stay mentally alert, give students a new perspective, assist students refocus from one learning activity to another, and provide students with an entertaining distraction when needed.

Exhibit 4.3 offers resources concerning mental and physical self-care and regular habits for instructors to share with students during course orientation. These resources can be added to the learning management system as embedded links, or Exhibit 4.3 can be used as a handout to distribute to students. Instructors should encourage students to make use of these resources as a way to fit self-care into their schedules.

In this chapter, we have suggested three support strategies for retaining students in online courses: instructional, institutional, and self-care. These strategies should be incorporated in the learning management system as embedded links that give students access to resources or as handouts. Close attention to the types of support services should be given when programs attract international students. The next chapter brings together the established findings and major contributions from our study related to online student retention. Chapter 5 offers a model for instructors to help students persist in an online course and explains how to put the model into practice. Chapter 5 discusses times of change for learning and instructors' skills for meeting students' 21st-century fluencies. The chapter ends with implications and conclusions for learning and teaching online.

Exhibit 4.3.
Self-Care Resources

Mental Habits

Everyday Mindfulness Exercises for Stress Relief: http://stress.about.com/od/tensiontamers/a/exercises.htm

10 simple mindfulness exercises: http://www.allconsidering.com/2009/10-mindfulness-exercises/

Mindfulness exercises: http://www.the-guided-meditation-site.com/mindfulness-exercises.html

Mindset—The New Psychology of Success: http://mindsetonline.com/

Meditation—A simple, fast way to reduce stress: http://www.mayoclinic.com/health/meditation/HQ01070

Learning Meditation: http://www.learningmeditation.com/

How to meditate: http://www.how-to-meditate.org/

Praying Each Day: http://www.prayingeachday.org/

10 Tips to Help Your Prayer Life: http://www.str.org/site/News2?page=NewsArticle&id=5648

Sacred Space—Your daily prayer online: http://www.sacredspace.ie

Physical Habits

Mayo Clinic exercise information: http://www.mayoclinic.com/health/exercise/HQ01676

WebMD—Pilates: http://www.webmd.com/fitness-exercise/features/the-benefits-of-pilates

WebMD—Yoga: http://www.webmd.com/balance/guide/the-health-benefits-of-yoga

Regular Habits

7 Steps to Effective Study Habits: http://www.make-or-break-habits.com/7-steps-effective-study-habits/

Importance of sleep: http://www.campusmindworks.org/students/self_care/sleep.asp

Realizations Inc.: Success Resources International: http://www.arlenetaylor.org/habits-addictive-behaviors/357-benefits-of-habits

Trusted.MD: http://trusted.md/blog/vreni_gurd/2009/04/25/exercise_improves_learning#axzz28j4uM4dB

Pulling the Strategies Together

In the first chapter of this book, we brought to your attention the changing higher education landscape and the institutional and instructional challenges that online education presents (Conceição & Lehman, 2011). For instance, the concepts of presence, communication, and interaction require rethinking on the part of the student and the instructor in the online environment. Also, due to changes in technology, online instruction, and online learning, the characteristics of the higher education student have been redefined and continue to be transformed. These changes make us think about the higher education landscape in a visual way: from brick-and-mortar, to brick-and-click, to click-link-and-connect.

The brick-and-mortar educational environment is clearly visible with its concrete buildings, physical campus setting, clear sense of time, close proximity for communication, well-defined boundaries, and face-to-face interactions with others. However, as higher education institutions start using technologies and adapting to these changes, institutions move toward a brick-and-click or a click-link-and-connect environment. This development requires being aware of and proactive about these changes by understanding the state of higher education and online learning and taking action to meet students' needs.

Based on reports (Allen & Seaman, 2010, 2011), the demand for online education is increasing and has an impact on enrollment in brick-and-mortar institutions. If institutions of higher education are not prepared to provide a successful online experience for students, student retention can be affected. Our goal in writing this book was to inform readers of the concerns and opportunities for online education and to provide research-based strategies for retaining students in online courses. In this chapter, we pull together the established findings and major contributions from our study, offer a model for online student retention, explain how to put the model into practice, discuss times of change for learning in the 21st century, identify challenges for teaching online in the 21st century, and present implications and conclusions for learning and teaching online.

ESTABLISHED FINDINGS RELATED TO ONLINE STUDENT RETENTION

In Chapter 1, we introduced Rovai's (2003) composite persistence model for retaining students in distance education online programs. This model identifies student external and internal factors that influence student retention in online programs. The external factors are related to nonschool issues that conflict with the student's academic life. The internal factors are associated with a student's needs and the services the institution provides to satisfy those needs. The institution has control over the interventions that can help meet students' needs. Students have some control over the internal factors through awareness and choice.

Studies have validated these factors. For example, Müller (2008) refers to external factors that influence student retention as load responsibility and motivation to complete a degree program; Park and Choi (2009) identify professional support; and McGivney (2009) finds that the desire to complete a degree is also an external factor. When it comes to internal factors that help with student retention, Tello (2007) states that students' attitudes have an impact on persistence. Park and Choi (2009) find that relevant course design reduces dropout rates, and Müller's (2008) studies show that lack of interaction with faculty, technology, and classwork influences a student's retention in online programs or courses.

MAJOR CONTRIBUTIONS FROM OUR STUDY

Our study on student motivation and support confirms many of the established findings and suggests new results. While Rovai's (2003) composite model is grounded in an institutional perspective and looks at a student's needs from a program standpoint, our study focuses on individual perceptions of learners from the online course experience and instructors' experiences with course design and support. Whereas Rovai's model views external and internal factors as what the institution can do for learners to meet their needs, our study uncovers intrinsic and extrinsic motivators from an individual standpoint.

Our study's major contributions are the strategies identified by students for staying motivated in online courses and strategies used by instructors for motivating and retaining online students. These strategies are based on the need to address the intrinsic and extrinsic motivators that can help guide students throughout the online course experience.

In our study, students identified as intrinsic motivators a purpose or small goals to persist in an online course or complete a degree program and extrinsic motivators as rewards that gave students a sense of satisfaction after completing their goal or goals. It was through time management, prioritizing, and learning strategies that students were able to meet their goals. Part of being motivated was to be self-aware of the learning process, the situation, and the consequences of not moving forward in an online course. In this process, students need to have self-value and a positive attitude to put into action a plan to complete the online course.

In our study, instructors' perspectives align with those of the students. The design strategies they identified as essential for motivating and supporting students in their online courses were strategies similar to those of the students. Instructors designed the learning environment with a structure that allowed students to manage their time, prioritize content, and use learning strategies that helped students stay motivated. The strategies used by instructors during the teaching process (setting up clear expectations, personalizing the online environment through interactions, and incorporating feedback throughout the course) created a sense of presence and were instrumental for students to achieve their course goals (intrinsic motivators) and receive academic, personal, or professional rewards (extrinsic motivators).

The majority of the instructors in our study were experienced online instructors (they had taught four or more courses). As a result of their experience, they could more easily predict learners' needs and preempt issues. Instructors used pre-course or orientation strategies that not only helped the students become familiar with the course, but also helped the instructors spend more quality time focusing on the content, interactions, and student learning, rather than on solving problems. Predicting learners' needs is an aspect of intentional design that decreases anxiety and frustration and enhances self-efficacy.

Two types of support strategies that are essential in online learning and teaching in higher education and that are increasingly being incorporated into course design are instructional and institutional support. Instructional support strategies are those provided by the instructor as part of the design of the course. Institutional support strategies involve available campus resources that help students succeed in the online course. A third type of support that emerged from our study and that is not commonly emphasized is self-care. This is important to students for staying motivated and having a balanced life. On the physical campus, students have close access to the gym, health center, physical activity classes, workshops for mindfulness, and so on. For online students, these resources may be available but are inconvenient due to distance or the requirement of an extra fee. In this case, online students may need to initiate their own self-care type of support. Often, online students' lives revolve around their school, work, and family, and self-care is neglected.

The findings of our study led to new ways of thinking about learning and teaching. Based on the demands of students' work, school, and personal lives, students prefer to take courses online for convenience, access, flexibility, efficiency, and cost savings. Taking courses online also provides students with an opportunity to stay current with 21st-century skills. The online environment allows students to gain an education anywhere, anytime, at any pace, and in any way they want with the use of desktop, mobile, and handheld technologies. This online environment encourages new ways of learning for students and a need for instructors to rethink how they teach and adapt to the demands of this changing environment.

NEW WAYS OF THINKING ABOUT LEARNING AND TEACHING

In the past, the traditional college student had a specific profile that was characterized by limited age range, socioeconomic status, and ethnicity, among other characteristics (Aslanian & Clinefelter, 2012; Dutton, Dutton, & Perry, 2002). We know that today online students have a different profile. As instructors, we need to be aware of these changes and focus instruction on the learner as a way to meet diverse needs.

We also know that students are learning in new ways due to technological advances (Small, Moody, Siddarth, & Bookheimer, 2009). Previously the focus on learning in higher education was on the left side of the brain (linear, logical, left to right, top to bottom, beginning to end, left-brain reading, writing, and numeracy). Today, we recognize that to survive in the 21st century, linear thinking is not enough. We need to think with the whole brain (Pink, 2005). Individuals need to be able to problem solve, use big-picture thinking, use their intuition and creativity, be able to synthesize information, and use emotional expression. For this reason, Jukes, McCain, and Crockett (2010) suggest that individuals should be fluent in problem solving, gathering and evaluating information, collaborating with others, being creative, and using media to analyze and interpret a message and to develop and publish artifacts.

New ways of learning lead to a new way of approaching teaching. This new way of teaching encompasses the whole mind. This means that learning outcomes should focus both on the left and right sides of the brain. In the past, instructors emphasized delivering content and testing out students' content knowledge through tests. This is one strategy for teaching. Today, with the availability of a variety of technologies, students can learn through discovery; problem solving; collaboration; digital product creation; and analysis, interpretation, and synthesis of facts, situations, and cases.

For the instructor, rethinking teaching strategies is one task. Learning how to use new technologies effectively is another task. Yet another task is shifting to teaching approaches that combine new strategies with emerging technologies and staying current with changes. However, using teaching strategies with technology effectively may not be sufficient for students. The context and relevance of the learning experience are needed for student retention. Based on our study findings, we developed the Persistence Model for Online Student Retention as a way for instructors to visualize what strategies students use for staying motivated and place an emphasis on how to better design the online environment, motivate students, and provide support.

PERSISTENCE MODEL FOR ONLINE STUDENT RETENTION

This book is written for instructors from both student and instructor perspectives. The main purpose of the book is to assist instructors when designing, teaching, and supporting the online experience of students. The strategies we present can help motivate and retain students as they progress through an online course. When

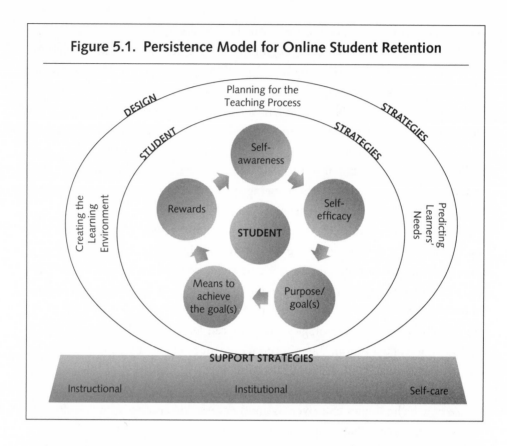

Figure 5.1. Persistence Model for Online Student Retention

Planning for the Teaching Process

DESIGN

STUDENT

STRATEGIES

STRATEGIES

Creating the Learning Environment

Predicting Learners' Needs

Self-awareness

Self-efficacy

Rewards

STUDENT

Means to achieve the goal(s)

Purpose/ goal(s)

SUPPORT STRATEGIES

Instructional

Institutional

Self-care

analyzing the student narratives, we noticed recurring patterns that students used to handle new information, issues, and behaviors. When comparing narratives to narratives and placing themes from these narratives into categories, we realized that these themes were moving in a path that in our view looked like a process. In this process, students identified clear strategies to keep them motivated in the online course. To explain the process and strategies, we offer the Persistence Model for Online Student Retention (Conceição & Lehman, 2012, 2013). Figure 5.1 illustrates the model. This model is student-centered (in other words, the model focuses on students' perceptions of how they proceed through an online course) and provides a context for instructors to design courses, teach, and support students online.

Student-Centered Model

The Persistence Model for Online Student Retention (Conceição & Lehman, 2012, 2013) is student-centered because the student is at the center of the online learning experience, has some control over the learning process, and takes responsibility for his or her own learning. Whereas in the traditional classroom the student can think, feel, and behave in a visible environment, online the environment is invisible. To make the experience seem real online, the student needs to be aware of the way the environment works, the process for learning, and the strategies needed to stay motivated when participating in an online course. By incorporating these strategies into the course, the instructor creates a sense of presence within the context of online learning and teaching.

Strategies for Helping Students Persist in an Online Course

When developing our persistence model, we consolidated the students and instructors' narratives into three categories of strategies: design, student, and support. The design strategies are the methods used by the instructor for incorporating intrinsic and extrinsic motivators into the online course. The student strategies provide a pathway for students to follow as they progress through their online learning experience. The support strategies are tools that help students meet their academic and personal needs.

Design Strategies   In the Persistence Model for Online Student Retention (Conceição & Lehman, 2012, 2013), the design strategies are placed in the outer sphere of the model and are the methods instructors use to incorporate intrinsic and extrinsic motivators into the online course. When the instructor is creating the learning environment, planning for the teaching process, and predicting learners' needs, the instructor takes specific strategies into account. When creating the learning environment, the instructor uses consistency, variety, relevance, and content prioritization to help students stay motivated throughout the course. When planning for the teaching process, the instructor sets up clear expectations, personalizes the interactions, and incorporates feedback throughout the course to create a sense of presence and engage students. To predict learners' needs, the instructor identifies students' skill deficiencies related to the course, lack of academic preparation for taking an online course, or inability to access resources before the course begins through student surveys, pre-tests, or learning analytics. As a result, the instructor can foresee challenges students may have in participating in the course and preempt problems that might occur.

Although in Figure 5.1 the design strategies may give the impression of being motionless, they are part of a dynamic process. In this dynamic process, the instructor must create the "big picture" of the course and at the same time intentionally develop the small details that make the elusive course feel real. Integrating a sense of presence in the teaching process by personalizing through interactions and incorporating feedback throughout the course can help students persist.

Student Strategies The inner sphere in Figure 5.1 contains student strategies that form a pathway for students to follow as they progress through their online learning experience. This pathway begins with a student's awareness of self, situation, and consequences. The pathway progresses to self-efficacy, which is the conviction of a student's own value and encompasses how a person thinks, feels, and behaves. Then, the pathway goes on to a purpose or goal to complete an online course because a goal or purpose provides the student with intrinsic motivation. To achieve the student's goal or goals, the student uses time management, prioritizing, and learning strategies. Finally, the student gains rewards after achieving this goal or goals in the form of extrinsic incentives. This process is cyclical as the student embarks in new online courses because each course may have its unique characteristics based on the discipline, format, interactivity, instructor role, technology, and support. By understanding this pathway, the instructor can incorporate intrinsic and extrinsic motivators into the course design and delivery.

Support Strategies Support strategies are the tools that the instructor can provide to students to help them meet their academic and personal needs. An online course may have strategic course design and engaging teaching strategies, but students may not feel that they are receiving sound support. If students are taking an online course for the first time, they will need assistance to prepare for the online learning experience. If students have remedial needs, for example in writing, to succeed in the course, they will need extra help to meet classroom standards of learning. If students have special needs such as being hard of hearing or sight impaired, they may need to use closed captioning software or screen readers. In these three cases, support strategies are very important for retaining students online. We have located the support strategies at the bottom of the model set out in Figure 5.1 because they are the base for giving students a sense of control over their learning (instructional support), making the environment conducive to learning (institutional support), and providing tools for self-reflection and self-awareness (student self-care).

Support is about instructor attention to students' needs. These needs may vary depending on students' characteristics and experience. Instructional support sets the framework for course interactions to occur and integrates a sense of presence into the course design. Having institutional support accessible within the course environment can show that the instructor is designing a student-centered course. Being aware of the importance of taking care of oneself and providing tips and resources to students on integrating mental, physical, and regular habits of self-care while taking the online course can benefit all in the learning process.

The online environment is elusive. To make this environment real and relevant for students, the context of the learning experience requires strategic design, a teaching process with a sense of instructor presence, and thoughtful support. In this case, the likelihood of students staying motivated online will be much higher.

Putting the Persistence Model for Online Student Retention into Practice The Persistence Model for Online Student Retention focuses on an individual experience within an online course. By being aware of the pathway students go through when taking an online course, instructors can strategically design their course and better develop supporting materials. Think of this model as a snow globe with a supporting base (support strategies). The student is at the center, like the object in the middle of the snow globe. The pathway the student goes through is transparent and unique for each student.

Now look at the elements of the pathway: self-awareness, self-efficacy, purpose or goals, means to achieve goals, and rewards. When you shake the globe, the elements come to life and are visible. The inside layer of the globe denotes the student strategies, which guide the student through the online learning process. Within the globe, there is a liquid environment for sustaining the process. The liquid symbolizes movement.

The outside surface of the globe, which is often made of glass, represents the design strategies that hold the globe together based on structure, process, and needs. The glass symbolizes fragility. The globe can be broken if its structures are not solid or on a firm base. If someone is not attentive and "drops the ball," the consequences can be overwhelming. Therefore, in order to be effective, the entire globe with its base needs to be in equilibrium. The same thing is true for online learning. A good base, strategic course design, and stable course process can provide a solid online learning experience for the student.

The strategies that emerged from our study were not new to us. However, incorporating them into a model was a way to place us as instructors in the role of the learner and visualize the learning and teaching process. Understanding the student perspective in an online course gave us a different sense of what it meant to learn online, especially for a novice learner in this environment.

When a student takes an online course for the first time, there is a lack of a sense of structure and a feeling of loss of control because of the boundless nature of the online environment. There is a need for the student to think about space, time, boundaries, use of the senses, and the levels of interaction in a different way. For these reasons, setting up clear expectations can enable novice students to create an image in their minds and sense of presence for the online experience. Often, we contact novice students proactively in the beginning of the course to find out how they are progressing, rather than waiting for them to contact us when there is a problem.

To help students stay motivated and persist, it is important for the instructors to learn about the students before the course begins. We often use a "Getting to Know You" survey, a pre-test of knowledge, a learning-style inventory, a survey assessing readiness for the online environment, and community-building activities. These strategies can be part of the course orientation prior to the beginning of the course or during the first week of the course and can preempt potential problems. In our courses, we also create "Clarifying Issues" and "Helping Each Other" discussion forums during the course to help reduce anxiety and frustration (Lehman & Conceição, 2010).

We also create course materials that help students overcome some of the challenges they face when taking an online course. It is important to remind students to review these course materials and direct them to the location of the documents within the course throughout the semester. For example, we have instructions on how to use various software programs, review document citation standards, examine sample projects, look over definition of terms, and so on. These resources can be introduced in the beginning of the semester but used later in the course. A reminder that the resources are available can diminish student anxiety.

Much of the student frustration in online courses is due to lack of self-control over academic and personal life. Our role as online instructors is to emphasize to students the importance of motivation and course planning when they take an online course. We need to remind students that they are in control over their lives and should self-manage their actions, accomplishments, and tasks. We have noticed that with time, students create or determine the most effective and efficient methods to accomplish course tasks.

To put the Persistence Model for Online Student Retention into practice, we suggest a checklist for instructors. Exhibit 5.1 provides a checklist for instructors

---

Exhibit 5.1.
Instructor Checklist for Designing Online Courses

When designing an online course, use the following checklist to identify tasks to accomplish:

___ Create a comprehensive syllabus containing instructor information, course description, course objectives, learning outcomes, required readings, course requirements and expectations, grading scale, course timeline, and institutional policies and procedures.

___ Develop the course structure, including consistency, variety, relevance, and content prioritization.

___ Plan for the teaching process by setting up clear expectations, personalizing the online environment, and incorporating feedback throughout the course.

___ Predict learners' needs by creating a course orientation that includes a *Getting to Know You* survey, a pre-test of knowledge, a learning-style inventory, a readiness for the online environment survey, and community-building activities.

___ Create guidelines for students to understand the online learning experience and the importance of student motivation when taking an online course.

___ Create a checklist of specific tasks students need to accomplish in the online course.

___ Provide students with "Netiquette" guidelines.

___ Insert links in the learning management system for electronic reserve, library, technical support, and student support services (writing center, special needs office, and counseling).

___ Insert links in the learning management system for mental, physical, and regular habits.

___ Create forums for non-content-related interactions (help desk, social, and virtual office hours) and content-related interactions (asynchronous and/or Web conferencing).

to design online courses. A comprehensive description on how to use the strategies in the checklist can be found in *Creating a Sense of Presence in Online Teaching: How to "Be There" for Distance Learners* (Lehman & Conceição, 2010).

TIMES OF CHANGE FOR LEARNING IN THE 21ST CENTURY

The 21st century is a time of change for learning that is allowing us to be creative and transformative because of the tools we have at our disposal and the interconnectivity created by these tools. Change happens organically, and today it is happening at a faster pace that involves internal and external factors affecting the daily lives of individuals. This organic process is the outcome of the dynamic interplay between the concrete world and the personal world of individuals. The higher education landscape is a part of the concrete world. In this concrete world, individuals have the ability to influence change. It is through transformation created by technology and adaptation that this organic change continues to evolve in the learning environment.

Learners in this changing environment are not just recipients of information. They play an active role in creating and managing their own knowledge, solving problems, collaborating with others, and sharing their expertise. This is no longer happening in a specific location with boundaries and time limitations. It is happening anywhere, anytime, at any place, and in any way that learners choose.

Learning is no longer restricted to a degree; learning has become a lifelong endeavor. It is also the learners' choice to use education in a way that is most beneficial to them. With technology changing exponentially, information and knowledge are now more fluid than ever and available to us in a matter of seconds. We can access information and explicit knowledge via the Internet through databases, websites, digital books, and electronic periodicals.

Unlike explicit knowledge, tacit knowledge comprises beliefs, ideas, and values and is more difficult to articulate, manage, and collaborate and share with others. Technology provides the means to develop and use tacit knowledge with others. In a changing environment driven by technology, individuals are required to gain new skills and new ways of learning to survive in school and the workplace. Instructors must be aware of the role they can play in helping students adapt to these changes and acquire new learning skills.

Instructors' Skills for Meeting Students' 21st-Century Fluencies

Today, the age range in higher education is limitless, socioeconomic status crosses a variety of levels, and students are from many ethnic backgrounds around the world. For instructors, the challenge is to become familiar with the diverse characteristics of these students. With technology changing almost daily and students entering college with advanced technology skills, there is a gap between instructors' and students' skills. This gap causes differences in expectations. To fill this gap, instructors must be continually updating their skills. Another challenge is to stay up-to-date on the use of new learning and teaching tools and shift teaching approaches to incorporate these tools and strategies that meet learners' needs for 21st-century fluencies.

However, meeting learners' needs for 21st-century fluencies requires that instructors acquire the following skills: course design management; working knowledge of digital educational materials; communication and facilitation; evaluation of digital products and interactions; and course workload management.

Course Design Management Skills   Creating an online course requires design skills and incorporating a sense of presence in online learning and teaching. The design skills include working knowledge of the process of determining the needs of the learner, identifying the goal of the course, and creating strategies to meet course goals. The course outcome should be measureable and attainable. There are many instructional design models in the literature that can be used to design an online course. Instructors can choose the one that best works for their specific situation.

In our first book together, we introduced a framework for designing online courses with a sense of presence (Lehman & Conceição, 2010). In this framework, we identify the determinants of presence (content, format, strategies, instructor role, technology, and support) as a way to strategically design the online course. Table 5.1 presents a blueprint for the Seminar in the Philosophy and History of Adult Education course. This blueprint example provides the "big picture" of the course and the detailed plan for course modules or units, readings, format, strategies, technology, and instructor role. This plan can be laid out in a variety of ways using flow charts, scripts, storyboards, timelines, software programs, and so on to depict the features of the course.

Table 5.1. Course Blueprint for the Seminar in the Philosophy and History of Adult Education

Module	Week	Readings	Format	Strategy	Technology	Instructor Role
Module 1: Course Overview	1	Elias & Merriam, Ch. 1 Stubblefield & Keane, Ch. 1 eReserve readings	Self-paced Group-based	Scavenger hunt Course introductions Student surveys Instructor welcome video	Welcome video Google Forms LMS Instructor Podcast eReserve	Facilitator Supporter
Module 2: Historical Perspectives	2, 3, 4	**Early Colonial and Early National** Stubblefield & Keane, Ch. 2–5 **National Growth and Social Divisions** Stubblefield & Keane, Ch. 6–9 **Urbanization, Industrialization, and Nationalization** Stubblefield & Keane, Ch. 10–12 eReserve Readings	Group-based	Instructor announcement Audio PowerPoints Asynchronous discussion Virtual office hours	Instructor Podcast LMS eReserve YouTube videos Website links PowerPoint Skype	Facilitator Observer Support Evaluator
Module 3: Historical Perspectives (continued)	5, 6, 7	**Depression, War, and Democracy** Stubblefield & Keane, Ch. 13–15 **Contemporary Issues** Stubblefield & Keane, Ch. 16–18 eReserve readings	Group-based	Instructor announcement Audio PowerPoints Asynchronous discussion Paper assignment due Colleague paper critique Mid-semester evaluation Virtual office hours	Instructor Podcast LMS eReserve YouTube videos Website links PowerPoint Skype	Facilitator Observer Support Evaluator

Module	Weeks	Topics / Readings	Format	Communication	Technology	Roles
Module 4: Philosophies of Adult Education	8, 9, 10	**Liberal Adult Education Philosophy** Elias & Merriam, Ch. 2; Merriam, Ch. 2 & 3 **Progressive Adult Education Philosophy** Elias & Merriam, Ch. 3; Merriam, Ch. 4–7 **Behavioral Adult Education Philosophy** Elias & Merriam, Ch. 4; Merriam, Ch. 8 & 9 eReserve readings	Group-based	Instructor announcement Audio PowerPoints Asynchronous discussion Virtual office hours	Instructor Podcast LMS eReserve YouTube videos Website links Powerpoint Skype	Facilitator Observer Supporter Evaluator
Module 5: Philosophies of Adult Education (continued)	11, 12, 13	**Humanistic Adult Education Philosophy** Elias & Merriam, Ch. 5; Merriam, Ch.10–13 **Radical Adult Education Philosophy** Elias & Merriam, Ch. 6; Merriam, Ch. 14–17 **Feminist Adult Education Philosophy** Merriam, Ch. 18 & 19 **Phenomenology Adult Education Philosophy** Merriam, Ch. 23 & 24	Group-based	Instructor announcement Audio PowerPoints Asynchronous discussion Virtual office hours	Instructor Podcast LMS YouTube videos Website links PowerPoint Skype	Facilitator Observer Supporter Evaluator

Continued

Table 5.1. Continued

Module	Week	Readings	Format	Strategy	Technology	Instructor Role
Module 6: Analytic Adult Education Philosophy, Evolving Directions in Adult Education and Paper Presentations	14, 15	**Analytic Adult Education** Elias & Merriam, Ch. 7; Merriam, Ch. 25–27 **Evolving Directions in Adult Education** eReserve readings	Group-based	Instructor announcement Audio PowerPoints Asynchronous discussion Paper assignment due Paper presentations Virtual office hours Final course evaluation	Instructor Podcast LMS eReserve Website links Audio PowerPoint Skype Qualtrics	Facilitator Observer Support Evaluator

Learning Management System (LMS) Feature Areas

Content

Discussion

Grading

Dropbox

Announcements

E-mail

Checklist

Surveys

Auxiliary Technology Tools

Library Electronic Reserve (eReserve)

Google Forms

YouTube

Podcast

Audio PowerPoints

Website links

Skype

Qualtrics for surveys outside the LMS

Working Knowledge of Digital Educational Materials Skills Incorporating digital educational materials into an online course requires a working knowledge of technology and selection of the appropriate technology tool for a given instructional situation. Learning how to use an educational technology requires hands-on and practice with the tool. Selection of the tool for the course involves matching the tool with the course goals and outcomes. For some institutions, instructional designers and media specialists do the actual development of the materials. For other institutions, the instructor "does it all." By having a working knowledge of available online resources, instructors can also incorporate existing digital educational materials that have already been developed into their courses. Web resources such as Merlot (http://www.merlot.org), TED (http://www.ted.com/), and Khan Academy (https://www.khanacademy.org/) provide valuable examples of digital educational materials available online.

Communication and Facilitation Skills In the face-to-face classroom, we take communication and facilitation skills for granted because they are a natural part of teaching. In the online environment, communication and facilitation require different skills. Instructors have to strategically plan for connecting and interacting with students to foster successful learning.

Communication in the online environment takes many forms using a variety of methods. Communication can be one-to-many through announcements, one-to-one through feedback, or many-to-many through cooperative or collaborative group discussion. Instructors can communicate using text, graphic, audio, or video formats. Online communication should be thoughtful, organized, concise, prompt, regular, encouraging, and constructive. Communicating in this way can motivate and guide students to a successful learning experience.

Facilitation in the online environment involves creating instructor presence by stepping back and encouraging students to take leadership, engaging students in in-depth conversations, soliciting active participation, and challenging students through questions. Facilitation means guiding learners and knowing when to intervene in the interactions. In our experience, we have seen that by understanding our students and observing their work patterns within the first weeks of the course, we can often predict their behaviors.

As students progress through the course, they become more engaged and independent. They also gain confidence and trust to work with others and rely less on us. The ability to balance our instructor presence is an important skill to create a successful learning experience. We encourage instructors to look at engaging strategies for online students in the book *Continuing to Engage the Online Learner: More Activities and Resources for Creative Instruction*, from our colleagues Rita-Marie Conrad and J. Ana Donaldson (2012).

Evaluation of Digital Products and Interactions Skills Some of the student assessment and evaluation skills used in the face-to-face classroom can be easily transferred to an online course, such as assessing content knowledge through tests, evidence of a skill through role play, or demonstration of a language skill through recitation. In the online environment, these types of assessment can also be easily done using a detailed rubric for presenting the skill and evaluating student performance.

For the evaluation of digital products, we believe in a process-based assessment that takes into consideration the learning development of the student throughout the course. For this reason, we divide the development of a digital product into a series of tasks. We provide feedback as tasks are completed and allow students to revise their work until the end of the course. In this way, we are looking at the developmental abilities of the student, rather than the product. We always tell our students that the process is more important than the product and that when the process is effective, the product will be too. This type of assessment provides students with opportunities to make mistakes as they learn and not be penalized for it.

For the evaluation of online interactions, in addition to assessing for basic thinking, we assess students for critical and creative thinking skills. In the online environment, we are able to more explicitly access and assess these skills through text transcripts, graphic charts or concept maps, and audio or video recordings. These interactions usually happen in a cooperative or collaborative setting in which students have the opportunity to share and construct knowledge with other course members. In our online courses, these opportunities arise when students participate in interactions with an authentic audience of their peers and exchange experiences and share different perspectives of a topic or situation. These activities not only create a sense of group presence, but also allow students to gain competence in applying content in a new way.

Course Workload Management Skills Course workload consists of the tasks that are to be accomplished before, during, and by the end of an online course. Instructor workload can be determined by time spent on these tasks based on tangible factors such as the number of learners in the course, the type and focus of content, the course format, the interactive strategies, the instructor role, the type of technology, and the type of support provided (Conceição & Lehman, 2011). The ability to manage course tasks and prioritize time is a valuable skill for instructors to find work-life balance when teaching online.

In our second book together, we introduced a template for managing tasks and prioritizing time (Conceição & Lehman, 2011) as a guide for balancing one's workload when creating an online course. The template can help instructors estimate the tasks and time spent during the design and delivery of the course. Table 5.2 provides an example of the template for managing tasks and prioritizing time as used in a seminar in the Philosophy and History of Adult Education. This example shows how to manage tasks and prioritize time for an existing course. This course was taught previously, and the instructor is revising dates and course materials. The number of hours would be much higher for designing and delivering a new course.

In our experience in working with other instructors, using the template has given both novice and seasoned instructors a new perspective on their teaching. As instructors reflected on using the template, one instructor realized that his emphasis has been mainly on course content rather than on interactions. Another instructor said that she became aware of the importance of pre-course preparation that would ensure that she had ample time to fully engage with students during the course. A third instructor shared how valuable it was to systematically document the tasks used to develop an online course in order to simplify the process, discover effective ways to complete the tasks, and use the template to train others.

Having a solid plan for an online course can create a conducive learning environment for students and be a time-saver for the instructors. For instructors, allocating appropriate time for course tasks can mean that instructors control their time, rather than time controlling them.

We, like many of our colleagues who responded to our study survey, have taught many online courses but often overlook our own professional development needs due to a rapidly changing higher education environment. It is

Table 5.2. Managing Tasks and Prioritizing Time for the Seminar in the Philosophy and History of Adult Education (Existing Course)

Course Sequence	Type of Task	Time Period/Time Spent
Before Course Begins	**Design**	**4 weeks before beginning of course**
	• Revise course resources list (readings, electronic reserve, and Internet resources)	3 hours
	• Copy the course structure in the learning management system (LMS) from a previous semester and update the files (syllabus, content area, discussion forums, Dropbox, checklist, campus resource links, grade book, and survey)	5 hours
	• Revise the six course modules' content and materials (audio PowerPoint presentations, YouTube and Web links), place them in content area of LMS, and schedule release time	10 hours
	• Finalize course decisions, ask someone else to review course for deadlines, expectations, clarity, and consistency.	2 hours
	• Create welcome announcements	1 hour
	Administrative	**2 weeks before first day of class**
	• Activate the course and send out welcome announcement via e-mail	3 hours, ongoing, as they occur
	• Respond to student clarification questions during orientation	
	• Provide technical support and respond to student e-mails	
		TOTAL HOURS BEFORE COURSE BEGINS: 24 hours

During and at End of Course	Design	Ongoing/daily
	• Journal ideas and thoughts for future changes in the course	3 hours for the entire semester
	Administrative	5 hours per week = 75 hours
	• Create announcements for each module to clarify issues and prepare students for upcoming modules	
	• Assign students into groups, create groups in LMS discussion area, and give students access to the designated group area	
	• Regularly manage the technology for broken links and release of LMS areas	
	• Use the LMS reports to monitor learner participation and course interactions	
	• Remind students of campus resources and provide technology support within the LMS	
	• Hold virtual office hours and respond to students e-mails and phone calls within a specific time	
	Facilitative	5 hours per week = 75 hours
	• Read postings and solicit students' comments and encourage participation during discussion	
	• Guide students in the course presentations	
	• Continue to share resources in discussion area	
	• Respond to questions on a regular basis	
	Evaluative	3 hours upon completion of a module = 18 hours
	• Provide individual feedback on papers	
	• Provide group feedback on discussions	
	• Grade module discussions and papers	
	• Conduct mid-semester evaluation	TOTAL HOURS BEFORE COURSE BEGINS: 168 hours, or an average of 11 hours a week

critical that as we are "there" for our students, we also need to take care of our professional needs. By establishing a systematic process for being open to recurring change, evaluating our current practices, and creating an ongoing professional development plan, we can enhance our practice and better meet students' needs. As a starting point, to create a professional development plan, we suggest that instructors look at the book *The Excellent Online Instructor: Strategies for Professional Development*, from our colleagues Rena M. Palloff and Keith Pratt (2011).

IMPLICATIONS AND CONCLUSIONS FOR LEARNING AND TEACHING ONLINE

Chapters 2, 3, and 4 provided strategies to design online courses, guide learning, and support online students. This chapter brought together these strategies and described the Persistence Model for Online Student Retention (Conceição & Lehman, 2012; 2013). These strategies and methods have practical implications for learning and teaching online. They can help students understand what it means to be an online learner and identify a pathway and strategies for successful online learning. These strategies and methods can help instructors design an online environment that meets students' needs, teach efficiently and effectively, and integrate support into online courses by creating an environment conducive to learning.

How can the model help the instructor guide the students to be successful online? While online learning may not serve everyone's needs, for students who are taking an online course for the first time, the instructor may use the model as a guide to help students think, feel, and behave in the online environment. In contrast, students who have taken more than one online course tend to be more perceptive about the online environment and may have greater insight about what it means to be an online learner. The instructor can use the model to guide the experienced online learner to identify more effective time management, prioritizing, and learning strategies to stay motivated throughout the course. To use these strategies all learners need to pre-plan, be organized, and have discipline. Students must also have a sense of self to stay on track.

How can the model help the instructor design, teach, and support students online? By understanding what it means to be an online learner, the instructor can develop the "big picture" of the course along with the smaller chunks that meet students' needs. By creating a course structure that is relevant and consistent, has variety, and prioritizes content in a way that is meaningful to the students, the instructor can help them navigate through the course in a more efficient and effective manner. By integrating support into online courses, the instructor can help the students become more self-aware, self-managed, self-disciplined, and self-directed.

The role of the instructor in this shifting higher education environment can influence how prepared students are for taking and persisting in online courses, succeeding in the workplace, and learning life skills. But instructors need to open their eyes and use their senses to realize what is going on in this changing world of technology, move with this change and be an integral part of it, and then act upon it. We hope that this book can help instructors visualize this change and take action that will impact the lives of their students.

Glossary

Any way education: With the proliferation of innovative technologies available today, students can learn any way they want. Students can take an online course using a smartphone, a tablet, a computer, a personal digital assistant (PDA), a global positioning system (GPS), a television, and so on.

Asynchronous: Participants do not need to be online at the same time. Information is posted and available to course participants on an "anytime, anywhere, any pace" basis.

Brick-and-mortar: The traditional higher education environment where learners live on campus and are present to others in a specific location, walk to classes, attend regular courses during normal working hours, participate in campus activities, communicate, socialize, and interact with other students and instructors within the confines of the campus area.

Brick-and-click: The traditional higher education campus environment where learners reside in campus housing, near campus, or commute with the advantages of the innovative use of technology.

Click-link-and-connect: A virtual campus environment composed solely of technology, where presence is elusive, communication is electronic, and interactions take place in cyberspace.

Course structure: One of the design elements for keeping students motivated in the online course. Structure includes consistency, variety, relevancy, and content prioritization as attributes for a successful online learning experience. These attributes provide the instructor with criteria on how to efficiently and effectively design the online course.

Consistency: The way the information in an online course is displayed and the regularity with which the information is presented.

Design strategies: Methods for structuring the course, planning for the teaching, and predicting learners' needs.

Extrinsic incentives: These incentives come from without, involve rewards, and decline in interest when the rewards are no longer present.

Fluencies: Skills needed to succeed in the new learning environment: solution, information, collaboration, creativity, and media (Jukes, McCain, & Crockett, 2010).

Growth mindset: The belief that the most basic abilities can be developed through dedication and hard work (Dweck, 2007).

Intentional course design: A method that involves purposeful actions and takes into consideration the online learning environment, the teaching process, and learner characteristics.

Intrinsic motivation: This comes from within (such as self-feedback) and is the most rewarding and long-lasting type of motivation.

Learning analytics: For this book, we use this term for the statistical reporting of data about students within the learning management system. These data provide information about students' connections within a course and help instructors predict and advise student learning.

Learning management system (LMS): Web-based software for delivering tracking, and managing online courses. The LMS also allows users to locate learning materials and activities related to online courses from any location with Internet access.

Learning strategies: These strategies are methods for learning content and procedures that influence students' study habits.

Persistence: The ability to continue decisively on a course of action in spite of difficulty or opposition.

Personalizing: Creating a warm feeling of presence and a conversational tone when developing materials that are in text, graphics, audio, or video formats.

Prioritizing: The process of organizing time, documents, tasks, and personal affairs in order of importance.

Relevant: When something is pertinent and applicable to learners' interests, workplaces, and lives.

Retention: The ability of an institution to retain students in an online program or course until completion.

Reward: Something that students receive after a goal has been achieved within an online course (academic reward), gives them pleasure after completing the course (personal reward), or helps them put into practice what they have learned (professional reward).

Self-efficacy: The conviction of one's value and capability to organize and put into action what is necessary to successfully move ahead to an end goal.

Self-management strategies: The methods and skills students used to achieve their goals.

Student strategies: Methods that keep students motivated when taking online courses.

Support strategies: Methods that create an environment conducive to learning (instructional), provide assistance for accessing campus resources and services (institutional), and encourage reflection and self-awareness of own strengths and weaknesses (self-support).

Synchronous: Participants are online at the same time of day using real-time technology environments, such as chat rooms or Web conferencing.

Time management strategies: The methods used by students to effectively and efficiently accomplish course tasks.

Variety: The means of including a mix of content (fact-based, process-based, or both), formats (self-paced, group-based, or both), and activities and technologies (synchronous, asynchronous, or both) when designing an online course.

References

Abel, R. (2005). *Achieving success in Internet-supported learning in higher education: Case studies illuminate success factors, challenges, and future directions*. Lake Mary, FL: The Alliance for Higher Education Competitiveness, Inc. Retrieved from http://www.msmc.la.edu/include/learning_resources/online_course_environment/A-HEC_IsL0205.pdf.

Allen, I., & Seaman, J. (2010). *Learning on demand: Online education in the United States, 2009*. Babson Park, MA: Babson Survey Research Group. Retrieved August 10, 2012, from http://www.sloanconsortium.org/publications/survey/pdf/learningondemand.pdf.

Allen, I., & Seaman, J. (2011). *Going the distance: Online education in the USA 2011*. Wellesley, MA: Babson. Retrieved from http://www.tonybates.ca/2011/11/09/online-enrollments-in-the-usa-grow-10-in-2011-oers-becoming-accepted/.

Angelino, L. M., Williams, F. K., & Natvig, D. (2007). Strategies to engage online students and reduce attrition rates. *The Journal of Educators Online, 4*(2).

Aslanian, C. B., & Clinefelter, D.L. (2012). *Online college students 2012: Comprehensive data on demands and preferences*. Louisville, KY: The Learning House, Inc.

Bandura, A. (1986). *Social foundations of thought and action: A social cognitive theory*. Englewood Cliffs, NJ: Prentice-Hall.

Bandura, A. (1996, April). *Assessing self-efficacy beliefs and academic outcome: The case for specific city and correspondence*. A paper presented at the annual meeting of the American Educational Research Association, New York, NY.

Bandura, A. (1997). *Self-efficacy: The exercise of control*. New York: W.H. Freeman.

Brown, R. E. (2001). The process of community-building in distance learning classes. *Journal of Asynchronous Learning Networks, 5*(2), 18–35.

Carr, N. (2011). *The shallows: What the Internet is doing to our brains.* New York: W. W. Norton & Company.

Carr, S. (2000). As distance education comes of age, the challenge is keeping the students. *Chronicle of Higher Education,* A39. Retrieved from http://chronicle.com/weekly/v46/i23/23a00101.htm.

Carroll-Barefield, A., Smith, S. P., Prince, L. H., & Campbell, C. A. (2005). Transitioning from brick and mortar to online: A faculty perspective. *Online Journal of Distance Learning Administration, 8*(1). Retrieved from http://www.westga.edu/%7Edistance/ojdla/spring81/carroll81.htm.

Chyung, S. Y., & Vachon, M. (2005). An investigation of the satisfying and dissatisfying factors in e-learning. *Performance Improvement Quarterly, 18,* 97–114.

Conceição, S. (2006). Faculty lived experiences in the online environment. *Adult Education Quarterly, 57*(1). American Association for Adult and Continuing Education.

Conceição, S.C.O., & Donohue, C. (August, 2012). *Intentional design based on understanding the learners, teachers, and content.* Proceedings of the Annual Distance Teaching and Learning Conference. Madison, Wisconsin.

Conceição, S.C.O., & Lehman, R. M. (2011). *Managing online instructor workload: Strategies for finding balance and success.* San Francisco: Jossey-Bass.

Conceição, S.C.O., & Lehman, R. M. (2012, November). *Motivation and support strategies for online adult learners in the 21st century.* American Association for Adult and Continuing Education. Las Vegas, NV.

Conceição, S.C.O., & Lehman, R. M. (2013, June). Persistence model for online student retention. *Proceedings of the Ed-Media Conference,* Victoria, British Columbia, Canada.

Conceição, S.C.O., & Schmidt, S. (2010). How non-content-related forums influence social presence in the online learning environment. *Indian Journal of Open Learning, 19*(2), 73–85.

Conrad, R., & Donaldson, J. A. (2012). *Continuing to engage the online learner: More activities and resources for creative instruction* (Online Teaching and Learning Series). San Francisco: Jossey-Bass.

Creswell, J. W. (1998). *Qualitative inquiry and research design: Choosing among five traditions.* Thousand Oaks, CA: Sage Publications.

Dabbagh, N. (2007), The online learner: Characteristics and pedagogical implications. *Contemporary Issues in Technology and Teacher Education, 7*(3), 217–226.

Diaz, D. P., & Bontenbal, K. F. (2001). Learner preferences: Developing a learner-centered environment in the online or mediated classroom. *Ed at a Distance, 15*(8).

Dutton, J., Dutton, M., & Perry, J. (2002). How do online students differ from lecture students? *Journal of Asynchronous Learning Networks, 6*(1).

Dweck, C. (2007) *Growth mindset: The new psychology of success.* New York: Ballantine Books.

EDUCAUSE (2011). *ECAR National Study of Undergraduate Students and Information Technology.*

Hara, N., & Kling, R. (2001). Student distress in web-based distance education. *Educause Quarterly, 3*, 68–69.

Hobbs, V. (2004). *The promise and the power of online learning in rural education.* Arlington, VA: Rural School and Community Trust.

Jukes, I., McCain, T., & Crockett, L. (2010). *Understanding the digital generation: Teaching and learning in the new digital landscape.* Thousand Oaks, CA: Sage.

Kinser, K., & Deitchman, J. (2007–2008). Tenacious persisters: Returning adult students in higher education. *Journal of College Student Retention: Research, Theory, and Practice, 9*(1), 75–94.

Lehman, R. M., & Conceição, S.C.O. (2010). *Creating a sense of presence in online teaching: How to "be there" for distance learners.* San Francisco, CA: Jossey-Bass.

Maguire, L. L. (2005). Literature review—faculty participation in online distance education: Barriers and motivators. *Online Journal of Distance Learning Administration, VIII*(I). Retrieved from http://www.westga.edu/%7Edistance/ojdla/spring81/maguire81.htm.

McGivney, R. J. (2009) *Adult student persistence in online education: Developing a model to understand the factors that affect adult student persistence in a course.* Open Access Dissertations, Paper 17. Available at http://scholarworks.umass.edu/open_access_dissertations/17.

Motteram, G., & Forrester, G. (2005). Becoming an online distance learner: What can be learned from students' experiences to distance programmes? *Distance Education, 26*(3), 281–298.

Muilenburg, L. Y., & Berge, Z. L. (2005). Student barriers to online learning: A factor analytic study. *Distance Education, 26*(1), 29–48.

Müller, T. (2008). Persistence of women in online degree-completion programs. *International Review of Research in Open and Distance Learning, 9*(2), 1–18.

Palloff, R., & Pratt, K. (1999). *Building learning communities in cyberspace: Effective strategies for the online classroom.* San Francisco, CA: Jossey-Bass.

Palloff, R., & Pratt, K. (2005). *Collaborating online: Learning together in community.* San Francisco, CA: Jossey-Bass.

Palloff, R. M., & Pratt, K. (2011). *The excellent online instructor: Strategies for professional development.* San Francisco, CA: Jossey-Bass.

Park, J., & Choi, H. (2009). Factors influencing adult learners' decision to drop out or persist in online learning. *Educational Technology & Society, 12*(4), 207–217.

Pink, D. H. (2005). *A whole new mind: Moving from the information age to the conceptual age.* New York: Riverhead.

Roblyer, M. D. (2006). *Integrating educational technology into teaching* (4th ed.). Upper Saddle River, NJ: Pearson Prentice Hall.

Rovai, A. P. (2003). In search of higher persistence rates in distance education online programs. *Internet & Higher Education, 6*(1), 1–16 (ERIC Document Reproduction Service No. EJ666602).

Rovai, A. P., & Wighting, M. J. (2005). Feelings of alienation and community among higher education students in a virtual classroom. *Internet & Higher Education, 8*(2), 97–110. (ERIC Document Reproduction Service No. EJ803728). Retrieved from http://dx.doi.org/10.1016/j.iheduc.2005.03.001.

Simpson, O. (2004). The impact on retention of interventions to support distance learning students. *Open Learning, 19*(1), 79–95.

Small, G. W., Moody, T.D., Siddarth, P., & Bookheimer, S. Y. (2009). Your brain on Google: Patterns of cerebral activation during Internet searching. *American Journal of Geriatric Psychiatry, 17*(2), 116–26.

Stanford-Bowers, D. (March, 2008). Persistence in online classes: A study of perceptions among community college stakeholders. *Merlot Journal of Online Learning and Teaching, 4*(1).

Svinicki, M. D. (2004). *Learning and motivation in the postsecondary classroom.* San Francisco, CA: Anker Publishing.

Tallent-Runnels, M. K., Thomas, J. A., Lan, W. Y., Cooper, S., Ahern, T. C., Shaw, S. M., & Liu, X. (2006). Teaching courses online: A review of the research. *Review of Educational Research, 76*(1), 93–135.

Tello, S. (2007). An analysis of student persistence in online education. *International Journal of Information and Communication Technology Education, 3*(3), 47–62.

Terantino, J. M., & Agbehonou, E. (2012). Comparing faculty perceptions of an online development course: Addressing faculty needs for online teaching. *Online Journal of Distance Learning Administration*, 15(2).

Waldrop, M. (2013, March 13). Massive Open Online Courses, aka MOOCs, transform higher education and science. *Scientific American*. Retrieved from http://www.scientificamerican.com/article.cfm?id=massive-open-online-courses-transform-higher-education-and-science&goback=.gmp_56349.gde_56349_member_222786807.

Ward, D. (2013, March 4). Online courses will extend UW-Madison to more students. *Wisconsin State Journal*. Retrieved from http://host.madison.com/wsj/news/opinion/column/guest/david-ward-online-courses-will-extend-uw-madison-to-more/article_9a20ec0a-82ba-11e2-89f6-0019bb2963f4.html.

Wlodkowski, R. J. (2008). *Enhancing adult motivation to learn: A comprehensive guide for teaching all adults* (3rd ed.). San Francisco, CA: Jossey-Bass.

Survey Questionnaire for Students

How did you find out about this study survey?

_____ Twitter

_____ Facebook

_____ LinkedIn

_____ Listserv

_____ eInterface website

_____ Referred by someone else

_____ Other: _____

Your discipline: _____

Type of courses you have taken: _____

_____ Undergraduate

_____ Graduate

Course duration (select all that apply):

_____ 4 weeks

_____ 6 weeks

_____ 8 weeks

_____ 15–16 weeks

_____ Other (please indicate duration):_____

Average number of students enrolled in your online courses:

_____ I was the only student

_____ Less than 10

_____ 11–20

_____ 21–30

_____ 31–50

_____ 51–100

_____ More than 100

_____ I don't know

How many online courses have you taken?

_____ 1

_____ 2

_____ 3

_____ 4 or more

Did your online courses include orientation activities?

_____ Yes

_____ No

_____ Some did

Please describe the activities you participated in during the course orientation:_____

What was the focus of your online courses? (please select all that apply)

_____ Process-focused (courses that focus more on process than content, such as group projects, team work, etc.)

_____ Content-focused (courses that focus primarily on content knowledge and discussion)

_____ Mix of content-focused and process-focused

_____ Other (please describe):_____

What formats were included in your online courses? (please select all that apply)

_____ Self-paced

_____ Group-based

_____ Mixed format including self-paced and group-based

_____ Other (please describe):_____

What interactive activities were included in your online courses? (please select all that apply)

_____ Case study in a group discussion

_____ Debates in a group discussion

_____ Guest speaker discussions

_____ Interviews

_____ Online asynchronous group discussions

_____ Role-play

_____ Online synchronous group discussions

_____ Virtual team projects

_____ Other (please describe):_____

What roles did your instructor play in your online courses? (please select all that apply)

_____ Catalyst (instigated conversations)

_____ Lecturer through video (provided lecture using PowerPoint and voice over)

_____ Facilitator of online discussions (participated and led discussions from the sidelines, clarified issues)

_____ Instructional designer (designed the online course)

_____ Mentor (guided students to succeed online through one-on-one meetings)

_____ Supporter (assisted students with special needs/disabilities)

_____ Tutor (helped students who were working independently on a self-paced mode)

_____ Observer (stayed in the background observing students and intervening when necessary)

_____ Other (please describe):_____

What technologies were available in your online courses? (please select all that apply)

_____ Blogs

_____ Learning management system (such as D2L, Blackboard, WebCT, and so on.)

_____ Podcasts

_____ Second Life

_____ Skype

_____ Twitter

_____ Web conferencing (such as Blackboard Collaborate, Live Meeting, WebEx, Net Meeting, and so on.)

_____ Other (please describe):_____

What types of feedback did you receive from your instructors? (please select all that apply)

_____ E-mail acknowledgement of assignments

_____ Discussion board feedback

_____ Group/team feedback for projects

_____ Individual student feedback on discussion participation

_____ Individual student feedback on assignments

_____ Role play for problem solving with the instructor

_____ Synchronous (live) feedback on role play or demonstration

_____ Other (please describe):_____

What support did you receive in your online courses? (please select all that apply)

_____ Assistance with adaptive technology

_____ Electronic office hours with instructor

_____ Faculty-initiated contact (via telephone, Skype, or chat)

_____ Help from the Tutoring Center

_____ Institution technical support (such as help desk)

_____ Live chat with a librarian to find resources

_____ Live interpreting via video relay (VR)

_____ Review of assignments from the Writing Center

_____ Step-by-step explanation of a software application by the help desk

_____ Support from academic adviser

_____ Support referrals/s from academic adviser

_____ Video announcement from instructor

_____ Other (please describe):_____

What strategies most motivate you to participate in your online courses? (please rate them in the order of preference, with 1 being the strategy most preferred)

_____ Concept mapping

_____ Games

_____ Group/team work

_____ Group/team feedback

_____ Group announcements

_____ Help forums where students help each other

_____ Student-facilitated discussions

_____ Limited number of modules or units

_____ Peer evaluation

_____ PowerPoint with narration

_____ Use of quizzes

_____ Video demonstrations by the instructor

_____ Other (please describe):_____

What strategies keep you motivated to learn in an online course? (please rate them in the order of preference, with 1 being the strategy most preferred)

_____ Using anything that allows me to practice connecting a term with its definition.

_____ Using graphics to illustrate the word or concept and its definition.

_____ Combining similar words to better organize meaning.

_____ Creating an example of a concept definition in my own words.

_____ Recognizing key ideas through online text headings in outline format.

_____ Organizing concepts through writing and sorting into related categories.

_____ Creating a concept map to recognize relationships among key ideas.

_____ Placing concepts in hierarchical grouping.

_____ Designing a flow chart to sequence concepts and connect them with each another.

_____ Watching other classmates as they apply the concepts and creating a mental model of the process.

_____ Identifying the details of a process that uses examples to illustrate common steps or characteristics of the concepts being learned.

_____ Connecting concepts in a process to personal examples.

_____ Putting versions of the process side by side to compare and contrast them.

_____ Looking for relationships through online text marker (a brief notation that gives information by displaying the text below the topic) to recognize concepts, sub-concepts, and cross links among concepts.

_____ Employing an organizer to compare and contrast assumptions, ideas, and evidence.

_____ Developing a flow chart or concept map to visualize relationships within the whole.

How often do you use the following strategies when you take online courses?

Strategy	Never				Sometimes			Always
Analyze what I have to do for the online course before it begins.	1		2	3		4		5
Set a specific learning goal before the course begins.	1		2	3		4		5
Set a specific time to work on the online course.	1		2	3		4		5
Identify course expectations in terms of learning and assignments before course begins.	1		2	3		4		5
Mark electronically or highlight the text when I read.	1		2	3		4		5
Ask myself questions before, during, and after studying.	1		2	3		4		5
Pause periodically to summarize or paraphrase what I've just studied.	1		2	3		4		5
Create outlines, concept maps, or organizational charts of how the ideas fit together.	1		2	3		4		5
Look for connections between what I am studying right now and what I've studied in the past.	1		2	3		4		5
Write down questions I want to ask the instructor.	1		2	3		4		5
Reorganize and expand on the notes I took during reading and online discussions.	1		2	3		4		5
Take breaks periodically to keep from getting too tired.	1		2	3		4		5
Make up my own examples for concepts I am learning.	1		2	3		4		5
Put things into my own words.	1		2	3		4		5

Strategy	Never		Sometimes		Always
Make vivid images of concepts and relationships among them.	1	2	3	4	5
Be sure I understand any example provided by the instructor.	1	2	3	4	5
Create concept maps and diagrams that show relationships among concepts.	1	2	3	4	5
Ask the instructor for more concrete examples and picture them in my mind.	1	2	3	4	5
Look for practical applications in real life settings for the things I'm learning.	1	2	3	4	5
After studying, meet with a partner to trade questions and explanations.	1	2	3	4	5
Write out my own descriptions of the main concepts.	1	2	3	4	5
Discuss the course content in my online group discussion forum.	1	2	3	4	5
Answer questions my online group discussion forum	1	2	3	4	5
Share course materials and received feedback with my online group.	1	2	3	4	5
Collaborate with classmates in virtual teams.	1	2	3	4	5
Make sure I can answer my own questions during studying.	1	2	3	4	5
Work with another student to question each other's ideas.	1	2	3	4	5
Keep track of things I don't understand and note when they finally become clear and what made that happen.	1	2	3	4	5

Continued

Strategy	Never		Sometimes		Always
Have a range of strategies for learning, so that if one isn't working I can try another.	1	2	3	4	5
Remain aware of mood and energy levels during study and respond appropriately if either gets problematic.	1	2	3	4	5

Please describe the strategies you use to keep you motivated in accomplishing your online course work.

Please describe how you structure your schedule to complete your online courses.

Tell what support strategies you use the most in your online courses.

Thank you for taking the time to complete the survey.

Survey Questionnaire for Instructors

How did you find out about this study survey?

_____ Twitter

_____ Facebook

_____ LinkedIn

_____ Listserv

_____ eInterface website

_____ Referred by someone else

_____ Other: _____

Your discipline: _____

Type of online courses you teach:

_____ Undergraduate

_____ Graduate

_____ Undergraduate and graduate

Course durations (please select all that apply):

_____ 4 weeks

_____ 6 weeks

_____ 8 weeks

_____ 15–16 weeks

_____ Other (please indicate duration):_____

Average number of students enrolled in your online courses:

_____ Less than 10

_____ 11–20

_____ 21–30

_____ 31–50

_____ 51–100

_____ More than 100

How many online courses have you taught?

_____ 1

_____ 2

_____ 3

_____ 4 or more

Do you include online course orientation in your courses?

_____ Yes _____ No

If yes, please select strategies you include in your course orientation:

Strategy

Students review what they have to do for the online course before it begins.

Students set a specific learning goal before the course begins.

Students set a specific time to work on the online course.

Students identify course expectations in terms of learning and assignments before course begins.

Students look for connections between what they are going to study in your online course and what they have studied in the past.

Encourage students to write down questions they want to ask you.

Provide specific timelines for completing tasks.

Ask students to make up their own examples for concepts they will be learning.

Ask students to put things into their own words.

What is the focus of your online courses?

_____ Process-focused (courses that focus more on process than content, such as group projects, teamwork, etc.)

_____ Content-focused (courses that focus primarily on content knowledge and discussion)

_____ Mix of content-focused and process-focused

_____ Other (please describe):_____

What formats do you include in your online courses?

_____ Self-paced

_____ Group-based

_____ Mixed format including self-paced and group-based

_____ Other (please describe):_____

What interactive activities do you include in your online courses? (please select all that apply)

_____ Case studies

_____ Debates

_____ Fishbowl (assigning students to groups in roles to expand perspectives on a particular topic or issue)

_____ Guest speaker discussions

_____ Interviews

_____ Online group discussions

_____ Role play

_____ Simulation

_____ Synchronous group discussions

_____ Virtual team projects

_____ Other (please describe):_____

What roles do you play in your online courses? (please select all that apply)

_____ Catalyst (instigated conversations)

_____ Facilitator of online discussions (participated and lead discussions from the sideline, clarified issues)

_____ Instructional designer (designed the online course)

_____ Lecturer through video (provided lecture using PowerPoint and voice-over)

_____ Mentor (guided students to succeed online through one-on-one meetings)

_____ Observer (stayed in the background observing students and intervening when necessary)

_____ Supporter (assisted students with special needs or disabilities)

_____ Tutor (helped students who were working independently in a self-paced mode)

_____ Other (please describe):_____

What technologies do you use in your online courses? (Select all that apply)

_____ Blogs

_____ Learning management system (such as D2L, Blackboard, WebCT, and so on.)

_____ Podcasts

_____ Second Life

_____ Skype

_____ Twitter

_____ Web conferencing (such as Elluminate, Live Meeting, WebEx, Net Meeting, and so on.)

_____ Other (please describe):_____

What types of feedback do you provide to your students? (Select all that apply)

_____ E-mail acknowledgements of assignments

_____ Discussion board feedback

_____ Group/team feedback for projects

_____ Individual student feedback on discussion participation

_____ Individual student feedback on assignments

_____ Role play for problem solving

_____ Synchronous (live) feedback on demonstration

_____ Other (please describe):_____

What support do you provide to your students in your online courses? (select all that apply)

_____ Electronic office hours

_____ Faculty-initiated contact (via telephone, Skype, or chat)

_____ Fast response to course issues that need to be clarified

_____ Prompt feedback on course assignments

_____ Rapid response to individual e-mails from students

_____ Supplemental tutoring

_____ Technical support for technology issues

_____ Video announcement

_____ Other (please describe):_____

Please select the strategies that you use to motivate your students to participate in your online course. (select all that apply)

_____ Audio PowerPoints of your lectures

_____ Concept mapping construction

_____ Games

_____ Group announcements

_____ Group/team feedback

_____ Group/team work

_____ Help forums where students help each other

_____ Student evaluation of each other

_____ Student facilitated discussions

_____ Limited number of modules/units

_____ Use of quizzes

_____ Video announcements

_____ Video to illustrate or demonstrate a concept

_____ Other (please describe):_____

When you design your online course, what strategies do you use to motivate your students? I have them (please select all that apply)

_____ Use learning objects or anything that allows them to practice connecting a term with its definition.

_____ Use graphics to illustrate a word and its definition.

_____ Combine similar words to better organize meaning.

_____ Create examples of concept definition in their own words.

_____ Recognize key ideas through online text headings in outline format.

_____ Organize concepts through writing and sorting into related categories.

_____ Create a concept map to recognize relationships among key ideas.

_____ Place concepts into hierarchical groupings.

_____ Design a flow chart to sequence concepts and connect them with each another.

_____ Watch other classmates as they apply the concepts and create a mental model of the process.

_____ Identify the details of a process that uses examples to illustrate common steps or characteristics of the concepts being learned.

_____ Connect concepts in a process to personal examples.

_____ Put versions of the process side by side to compare and contrast them.

_____ Look for relationships through online text markers to recognize concepts, sub-concepts, and cross links among concepts.

_____ Employ an organizer to compare and contrast assumptions, ideas, and evidence.

_____ Develop a flow chart or concept map to visualize relationships within the whole.

Please describe the strategies that you perceive keep your students motivated in accomplishing the work in your online courses.

Please describe how you structure your course to incorporate motivation strategies in your online courses.

Please describe how you structure your course to incorporate support strategies in your online courses.

Thank you for taking the time to complete the survey.

Index

Page references followed by fig indicate an illustrated figure; followed by *t* indicate a table; followed by *e* indicate an exhibit.

Goals: means for achieving online course, 42–53, 60t–62t; or purpose for taking online course, 41–42, 60t; types of rewards for achieving, 53–56, 62t

Green learning environment, 10, 11

Group feedback, 28, 74t

"Growth mindset," 58

H

Hara, N., 5

Help desk, 69

Higher education: causes for increased enrollment in, 3–4; current state of online learning in, 4–5; online innovation of, 1. *See also* Online education

Higher education environment: brick-and-click, 2, 11; brick-and-mortar, 2, 11, 83–84; click-link-and-connect online, 2, 11; creating learning opportunities through online, 10–11

Hobbs, V., 5

Human resource support: description of, 66; family and friends as, 68; instructor role in, 66–67; Persistence Model recommendations for, 90–91; role of peers in, 67–68

I

Icebreakers, 74t

Institutional services, 75, 79

Institutional support: accessibility to, 69–70; description of, 69; institutional services, 75, 79; instructional services, 75, 77, 79; Persistence Model recommendations for, 90–91; student services, 77–79, 80; technology support, 69

Instruction: chunking technique used in, 24; incorporating feedback into, 28–30, 36t–37t, 74t; providing consistency in, 21; relevance of, 22–24, 35t–36t; thinking about new approaches to, 87; using variety of, 21–22, 35t–36t. *See also* Teaching process

Instructional services, 75, 77, 79

Instructional support strategies: examples of, 72–73, 74t; for online courses, 74t;

Persistence Model recommendations for, 90–91; related to administrative tasks, 73

Instructor Checklist for Designing Online Courses, 93e–94

Instructors: emphasizing motivation and course planning to students, 92–93; how students are motivated by positive attitude of, 58–59; human resource support role by, 66; incorporating regular course feedback from, 28–30, 36t–37t, 74t; instruction assistance and participation by, 6; Instructor Checklist for Designing Online Courses for, 93e–94; need to develop collaboration fluency by, 13; personalizing online interactions with, 26–28, 36t–37t; setting up clear expectations for students, 25–26, 36t–37t; skills for meeting students' 21st-century fluencies, 95; strategies for motivating students, 6, 38–64e; synchronous meetings or virtual office hours held by, 27

Intentional online course design: description and examples of, 19–20; to help students stay motivated, 20–32; impact on online course success by, 32–34; relationship between student satisfaction and, 34; retaining online students through strategies of, 34–37t

Intrinsic motivation: barriers to, 6–7; incentives for, 57; Persistence Model design strategies to facilitate, 89; student-identified, 85. *See also* Online student rewards

J

Jukes, I., 13, 87

K

Khan Academy, 99

Kling, R., 5

Knowledge: explicit, 94; tacit, 94

L

Learners: predicting needs of, 30–32, 37t, 86; redefining the characteristics of higher education, 2. *See also* Online students

Learners' needs: ensuring course resources are accessible, 31, 37*t*; frequently asked questions (FAQs) to help meet, 31, 32, 69; identifying student skill deficiencies, 31, 37*t*; providing student orientation for, 30–31, 37*t*, 80; student self-efficacy enhanced by anticipation of, 86

Learning: implications and conclusions for teaching online and, 104–105; as lifelong endeavor, 94; more technologies providing new ways of, 2–3; thinking about new ways for teaching and, 86–87; 21st century as times of change for, 94–104

Learning environment: consistency attribute of the, 21, 35*t*–36*t*; content prioritization attribute of the, 24–25, 35*t*–36*t*; created through the course structure, 20–21; green, 10, 11; relevance of the, 22–24, 35*t*–36*t*; strategies for creating the, 35*t*–36*t*; 21st century changes for the, 94–104; variety attribute of the, 21–22, 36*t*–36*t*

Learning skills for the 21st century: communication and facilitation skills, 99–100; course design management skills, 95; course workload management kills, 101–104; evaluation of digital products and interactions skills, 100; instructors for meeting students' 21st-century fluencies, 95; requirements for developing, 94; Seminar in the Philosophy and History of Adult Education course example of applying, 95, 96*t*–98*t*, 101, 102*t*–103*t*; working knowledge of digital educational materials, 99

Learning strategies: GAMES model for efficient, 49–53; as means to achieve online course goals, 48–49; summary of specific, 64*e*; ways to incorporate in course design, 62*t*

Lehman, R. M., 1, 4, 10, 11, 14, 17, 18, 20, 73, 83, 88, 89, 92, 95, 101, 104

M

Maguire, L. L., 4

McCain, T., 13, 87

McGivney, R. J., 9, 84

Means to achieve goals: learning strategies, 48–50, 62*t*, 64*e*; prioritizing strategies, 46–48, 61*t*; setting schedule based on deadlines, 44–45, 60*t*–61*t*; setting schedule based on life roles and tasks, 45–46, 60*t*–61*t*; time management strategies, 42–43, 60*t*–61*t*, 63*e*; ways of incorporating into course design, 60*t*–61*t*

Media influence, 13

Merlot, 99

Monitoring student process, 74*t*

MOOCs (Massive Open Online Courses): flexible degree programs that integrate, 4; introduction into online higher education of, 12–13

Moody, T. D., 86

Motivation: design elements and strategies to support student, 20–32; explaining study findings from perspective of students, 56–59; GAMES model study on student, 50–53; how a learning community approach facilitates, 9; human resource support of, 66–68; institutional support of, 69–70; instructor emphasis to students on importance of, 92–93; intrinsic and extrinsic, 6–7, 57, 85, 89; self-care role in, 70–71; study on strategies for facilitating student, 6, 38–64*e*. *See also* Online student persistence; Online students

Motivation strategies: explaining study findings from motivational perspective, 56–59; incorporating them into course design, 59–62*t*; institutional support strategies, 75–80; instructional support strategies, 72–74*t*; instructor contact and assistance, 6; learning strategies, 48–53, 62*t*, 64*e*; means used by students to achieve goals, 42–53, 61*t*–62*t*; prioritizing strategies, 46–48, 61*t*, 63*e*; purpose for taking a course, 41–42, 60*t*–61*t*; rewards obtained by students for achieving course goals, 53–56, 62*t*; self-awareness, 39–40, 60*t*; self-care strategies and resources, 80–82*e*; self-efficacy, 40–41, 60*t*, 86; time

management strategies, 42–46, 60*t*–61*t*, 63*e*.
See also Online student retainment strategies

Motteram, G., 6, 59

Muilenburg, L. Y., 6, 7, 59, 65

Müller, T., 9, 84

N

Natvig, D., 5

O

Online announcements, 28

Online course completion predictors, 9–10.
See also Online student drop-out rates

Online course design: for consistency and variety, 21–22, 36*t*–36*t*; for content prioritization, 24–25, 35*t*–36*t*; for creating the learning environment, 20–21; creating the learning environment, 20–21; incorporating digital educational materials into, 99; incorporating feedback throughout the course, 28–30, 36*t*–37*t*, 74*t*; incorporating motivating strategies into, 60*t*–62*t*; Instructor Checklist for Designing Online Courses for, 93*e*–94; intentional approach to, 19–20; learning strategies in, 48–53, 62*t*, 64*e*; Persistence Model for Online Student Retention strategies for, 89–90, 93*e*–94; Persistence Model strategies for, 89–91; for personalizing the online environment through interactions, 26–28, 36*t*–37*t*; planning for the teaching process in the, 25, 36*t*–37*t*; predicting learners' needs aspect of, 30–32, 37*t*, 86; prioritizing strategies incorporated in, 46–48, 61*t*, 63*e*; purpose for taking a course incorporated in, 41–42, 60*t*–61*t*; relationship between student satisfaction and intentional, 34; for relevance, 22–24, 35*t*–36*t*; for retaining online students, 34–37*t*; rewards for achieving course goals incorporated into, 53–56, 62*t*; Seminar in the Philosophy and History of Adult Education course example of, 95, 96*t*–98*t*; setting up clear expectations, 25–26, 36*t*–37*t*; student

self-awareness and self-efficacy supported by the, 39–41, 60*t*, 86; time management strategies incorporated into, 42–46, 60*t*–61*t*, 63*e*; 21st-century skills required for, 95; understanding requirements for, 17–19

Online course goals: means of achieving, 42–53, 60*t*–62*t*; purpose for taking the course, 41–42, 60*t*; types of rewards for achieving, 53–56, 62*t*

Online courses: impact of intentional design for the success of, 32–34; implications and conclusions for teaching and learning in, 104–105; incorporating digital educational materials into, 99; intentional design for, 19–20; MOOCs (Massive Open Online Courses), 4, 12–13; purpose for taking, 41–42, 60*t*; Seminar in the Philosophy and History of Adult Education course example of, 95, 96*t*–98*t*, 101, 102*t*–103*t*

Online education: factors for student persistence in, 7–10; green environment of, 10, 11; implications and conclusions for teaching and learning in, 104–105; increasing demand for higher education, 4–5; increasing development and use of, 1; opportunities for, 10–22. *See also* Click-link-and-connect education environment; Higher education

Online environment: click-link-and-connect, 2, 11; comparing face-to-face classroom and, 17–19; factors distinguishing the, 18*t*; "green," 10, 11; intentional design of the, 19–32; personalizing interactions in the, 26–28, 36*t*–37*t*

Online student drop-out rates: common reasons for, 8*t*; faculty-student contact and assistance impact on, 6. *See also* Motivation; Online course completion predictors

Online student persistence: how a learning community approach facilitates, 9; student character and skills as factors in, 7–8; student's perspective as factor in, 8; studies on predictors of, 9–10. *See also* Motivation; Persistence Model for Online Student Retention

Prince, L. H., 2

Prioritizing strategies: as means of achieving online course goals, 46–48; ways of incorporating into course design, 61t

Professional rewards, 55–57, 62t

Psychological and emotional assistance, 74t

R

Ravai, A. P., 9

Relevance: designing course, 22–23; examples of course, 23–24; now to integrate into course design, 35t–36t

Remedial instruction services, 79

Rewards. *See* Online student rewards

Roblyer, M. D., 5

Rovai, A. P., 5, 7, 10, 59, 84

S

Seaman, J., 3, 4, 5, 83

Second Life, 67–68

Self-awareness: description of, 60t; staying motivated for online course factor of, 39–40; ways to incorporate into course design, 60t

Self-care: description of, 70; mental habits and resources for, 80–81, 82e; physical habits and resources for, 81, 82e; regular habits and resources for, 81, 82e; student stories on, 70–71

Self-efficacy: anticipation of learners' needs as enhancing, 86; description of, 60t; staying motivated for online course factor of, 40–41; ways to incorporate into course design, 60t

Self-value, 58

Seminar in the Philosophy and History of Adult Education course: design blueprint for the, 95, 96t–98t; template for managing tasks and prioritizing time for the, 101, 102t–103t

Setting expectations: teaching strategy of, 25–26; ways to integrate into course design, 36t–37t

Setting schedules: based on life roles and tasks, 45–46; using deadlines for, 44–45, 60t–61t; instructor emphasis to students

on importance of, 92–93; time management through the use of, 42–43, 44–45, 60t–61t, 63e; ways to incorporate into course design, 60t–61t. *See also* Course workload management

Siddarth, P., 86

Simpson, O., 5, 6

Small, G. W., 86

Smartphones, 10, 12

Smith, S. P., 2

Student enrollment: how demand for online education is impacting, 83–84; increase rates of, 3–4

Student orientation, 30–31, 37t, 80

Student services: description of, 77; EriksonOnline, 77, 78e–79e; types of, 80

Student skill levels: as barrier to online learning, 6; developing 21st century learning skills, 94–95, 99–101, 104; pre-admission, 7

Students: causes for increased enrollment of, 3–4; EDUCAUSE data on technology ownership and use by, 11–12; new learner behaviors and skills of, 11–14. *See also* Online students

Support strategies: human resource support, 66–68, 90–91; institutional, 68–80, 90–91; instructional, 72–73, 74t, 90–91. *See also* Technical support

Svinicki, M. D., 49, 52

Syllabus: looking at the "big picture" when creating, 19; setting clear expectations in the, 26, 36t–37t

Synchronous meetings, 27

T

Tablets, 10, 12

Tacit knowledge, 94

Tallent-Runnels, M. K., 5

Teaching process: incorporating feedback into, 28–30, 36t–37t, 74t; planning for the, 25; setting up clear expectations as part of, 25–26, 36t–37t; thinking about new approaches to the, 87; ways to integrate into course design, 36t–37t. *See also* Instruction

Technical support: FAQs, help forums and documents for, 31, 32, 69; frequently asked questions (FAQs) as, 31, 323; help desk, 69; as instructional support strategy, 74*t*; online tutorials, 69; supporting student technical skills through, 7–8. *See also* Support strategies

Technology: educational challenges due to new, 13; EDUCAUSE data on student ownership and use of, 11–12; instructional support related to, 72–74*t*; new ways of learning made possible through, 2–3; offering online education opportunities, 10–11; PASS (Panther Academic Support Services), 75, 76*e*; virtual environment, 67–68

TED, 99

Tello, S., 8, 84

Terantino, J. M., 32

Testing student services, 79

Time management strategies: achieving online course goals using, 42–43; description of, 60*t*; summary of specific, 63*e*; ways to incorporate into course design, 60*t*–61*t*. *See also* Course workload management skills

Tutorials, 31

21st century learning skills: communication and facilitation, 99–100; course design management, 95; course workload

management, 101–104; instructors for meeting students' 21st-century fluencies, 95; requirements for developing, 94; Seminar in the Philosophy and History of Adult Education course example of applying, 95, 96*t*–98*t*, 101, 102*t*–103*t*; working knowledge of digital educational materials, 99

U

University of Wisconsin Flexible Option, 12

University of Wisconsin-Milwaukee's Panther Academic Support Services (PASS), 75, 76*e*

V

Vachon, M., 6, 65

Variety: learning environment design aspect of, 21–22; ways to integrate into course design, 35*t*–36*t*

Virtual office hours, 27

W

Waldrop, M., 13

Ward, D., 4, 12

Welcome letter, 74*t*

Wighting, M. J., 5

Williams, F. K., 5

Wlodkowski, R. J., 58